P9-EMP-722

ENCOUNTERING PAUL

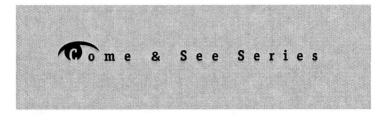

Come & See Series

The **Come & See Series** from Sheed & Ward is modeled on Jesus' compassionate question, "What do you seek?" and his profound invitation to "Come and see" the world through the eyes of faith (John 1:38–39). The series offers spiritual seekers lively, thought-provoking, and accessible books that explore topics of faith and the Catholic Christian tradition. Each book in the series is written by trustworthy guides who are the very best teachers, theologians, and scholars.

Series Editors: James Martin, S.J., and Jeremy Langford

People of the Covenant: An Invitation to the Old Testament
By Dianne Bergant

Who Is Jesus? Why Is He Important?: An Invitation to the New Testament
By Daniel Harrington, S.J.

Living Justice: Catholic Social Teaching in Action
By Thomas Massaro, S.J.

Professions of Faith: Living and Working as a Catholic
Edited by James Martin, S.J., and Jeremy Langford

A Faith You Can Live With: Understanding the Basics
By John O'Donnell

Bread of Life, Cup of Salvation: Understanding the Mass
By John Baldovin, S.J.

How Do Catholics Read the Bible?
By Daniel J. Harrington, S.J.

Simple Ways to Pray: Spiritual Life in the Catholic Tradition
By Emilie Griffin

Encountering Paul: Understanding the Man and His Message
By Tatha Wiley

ENCOUNTERING PAUL

Understanding the Man and His Message

Tatha Wiley

A Sheed & Ward Book

ROWMAN & LITTLEFIELD PUBLISHERS, INC.

Lanham • Boulder • New York • Toronto • Plymouth, UK

A Sheed & Ward Book
Published by Rowman & Littlefield Publishers, Inc.
A wholly owned subsidiary of
The Rowman & Littlefield Publishing Group, Inc.
4501 Forbes Boulevard, Suite 200, Lanham, Maryland 20706
http://www.rowmanlittlefield.com

Estover Road, Plymouth PL6 7PY, United Kingdom

Copyright © 2010 by Tatha Wiley

All rights reserved. No part of this book may be reproduced in any form or by any electronic or mechanical means, including information storage and retrieval systems, without written permission from the publisher, except by a reviewer who may quote passages in a review.

British Library Cataloguing in Publication Information Available

Library of Congress Cataloging-in-Publication Data

Wiley, Tatha.
  Encountering Paul / Tatha Wiley.
      p. cm. — (Come & see series)
  "A Sheed & Ward book."
  Includes index.
  ISBN 978-0-7425-5808-3 (cloth : alk. paper) — ISBN 978-0-7425-5809-0 (pbk. : alk. paper) — ISBN 978-1-4422-0199-6 (electronic)
  1. Bible. N.T. Epistles of Paul—Criticism, interpretation, etc. 2. Paul, the Apostle, Saint. I. Title.
  BS2650.52.W55 2010
  227'.06—dc22   2009034293

♾™ The paper used in this publication meets the minimum requirements of American National Standard for Information Sciences—Permanence of Paper for Printed Library Materials, ANSI/NISO Z39.48-1992.

Printed in the United States of America

To my mother—
like Paul,
a traveler
and
an independent spirit

Contents

Preface

The Apostle Paul is one of the most fascinating and enigmatic figures in the first-century Jesus movement. His influence has been so profound that Christianity itself has often been called Pauline Christianity.

For centuries, theologians and biblical scholars have pored over Paul's letters to draw out his understanding of the significance of Jesus of Nazareth. Of the historical Jesus we learn very little from Paul. Yet it is this Jesus' death that is at the center of Paul's religious worldview. God raised the crucified Jesus to new life. This is what is of paramount interest to Paul.

Paul's idea that we "belong" to the risen Jesus has been the subject of countless sermons and theological treatises. Paul's theme that justification is by faith in Jesus alone even spawned the Reformation and continues today to separate Catholic and Protestant communions. But Catholics as well as Protestants consider Paul's idea one of the primary convictions of Christianity itself.

Christian theology took its most distinctive terms and beliefs from Paul's letters. He is surely one of the most complex personalities in the New Testament. His letters offer a glimpse into both this personality and the dynamics of the assemblies of Gentile women and men founded by him around the Mediterranean world.

Throughout the tradition, interpreters read Paul as if he were writing abstract theological treatises on grace or salvation. But he wrote letters, responses to concrete problems, questions, and conflicts of real persons in real situations. What he said in response to a problem was the product of thinking something out on the spot. When he addressed the Thessalonians' anxiety about whether their dead members would share in the promised resurrection life, for example, his theology of bodily resurrection emerged at that time and in response to that particular question.

Modern scholars take the fact that Paul wrote letters and not theological treatises seriously. These are occasional writings, crafted hurriedly in jails and workplaces, addressed to people Paul wanted to influence with the only tool he had, the power of rhetoric. For one reason or another, he could not be with these communities to deal directly with problems as they presented themselves. All letters are relational, and Paul's are no exception. The text stands between the audience who has the problem, question, or conflict and the writer who formulates a response to their difficulty. Paul's overarching goal was to keep believing assemblies committed to the lives of holiness and justice to which he had introduced them through the transforming presence of the risen Lord in their midst.

Without Paul's letters we would have little clue about the diversity of the early Jesus movement, the enthusiasm of Spirit-filled communities, and the egalitarian ethic of redemption marked by the sharing of roles and functions within these communities (1 Cor 12; Gal 3:28).[1] The problems Paul confronted vary widely—they are constituted by disagreements over practices, divisions and factions, and sexual indiscretions.

One problem stands at the center of the collection of Paul's letters. It was not a problem on the side of an assembly but Paul's own. This was the challenge to his gospel, that is, the rejection by some of Paul's way of understanding the inclusion of Gentile women and men into the biblical promises given to Israel. This challenge was from within the Jesus movement, not from persons outside the movement. The conflict in Galatia was between these opponents and Paul over the conditions he had given to Gentiles for their inclusion in the eschatological Israel.

THE PAUL PRESUMED

Who was Paul? What do we know about him? At the onset, we should outline what we presume about him. Leaving the task of documentation for later, here is what we take to be the Paul of the New Testament letters.

What we know about Paul comes from two New Testament sources: first, his own letters, and second, the Acts of the Apostles. The writer of the Gospel of Luke is the writer of Acts. If there is a conflict between the letters and Acts, more weight is given to Paul's letters and his autobiographical remarks than to Acts.

Paul is thought to be from the city of Tarsus in Asia Minor. We have nothing to the contrary on his place of origin but no further verification of it either. He says nothing about his family or friends. Apparently he was not married. Paul's family may have had Roman citizenship. This would not be unheard of for a Jew in the Roman Empire, but, on the other hand, because Roman citizenship is attributed to him in Acts, it may have more to do with Luke's interests than strictly Paul's actual biography.

Paul's family is associated by Luke with the Pharisaic movement. Paul's writing suggests a good education, perhaps with Pharisees, but probably not with the famous Rabbi Gamaliel, as Luke says in Acts.

Paul was likely not educated in Jerusalem. He was a Hellenized Jew, located in the Diaspora (the Jews dispersed beyond Judea) and educated in Greek literary conventions. He did not speak Aramaic, as did Jesus, but Greek.

Paul identified himself with the Pharisees, and his "conversion" was a shift in allegiance from one Jewish party to another, from the Pharisees to a messianic group, the Jesus followers. His conversion was a mystical experience of the risen Jesus in which he was called to extend God's offer of salvation to the Gentiles. He claimed apostolic status on the basis of this experience: he had seen the risen Jesus.

Paul's message was eschatological. That is, Paul was convinced that the death and resurrection of Jesus signaled the beginning of the "end time" and God's end to the reign of evil that has distorted creation. He lived an intense spiritual life, apparently as a Pharisee early on, and then as a Jesus follower. His writing shows deep experiential insight into the human condition and into the meaning of divine redemption.

Paul became an evangelist in the Jesus movement, traveling over a wide area of the Roman Empire and, where people were receptive, establishing assemblies of Christ-professing believers. His preaching was exclusively directed toward non-Jews, Gentiles as they were called by Jews. Many scholars believe these Gentiles were "God-fearers," persons already drawn to Judaism but who had not yet undergone full conversion.

Paul's relationship with other Jesus followers, especially those in Jerusalem close to the historical Jesus, was somewhat uneasy. He was actively opposed by Jesus followers who disagreed with his position that Gentiles do not have to become Jewish to share in Israel's salvation.

Imprisoned several times, Paul's life ended in prison. He was killed in Rome by the imperial government, perhaps at the direct order of the emperor, Nero.

Some of the letters attributed to Paul were actually written several decades after Paul. Without Paul's own letters, we would not have a glimpse of Paul's missionary life or a sense of what belonging to Christ meant to him. To show the way in which belonging to Christ entails suffering, Paul gives a particularly graphic description of his life on the road to the Corinthians:

> Three times I was beaten with rods. Once I received a stoning. Three times I was shipwrecked; for a night and a day I was adrift at sea; on frequent journeys, in danger from rivers,

danger from bandits, danger from my own people, danger from
Gentiles, danger in the city, danger in the wilderness, danger
at sea, danger from false brothers and sisters; in toil and hard-
ship, through many a sleepless night, hungry and thirsty, often
without food, cold and naked. And, besides other things, I am
under daily pressure because of my anxiety for all the churches.
(2 Cor 11:25–28)

THREE ARGUMENTS

Generations of Christians have found Paul's letters powerful and insightful. But his influence has not been without
its problematic aspects. While many have found his words
liberating, others have experienced them as oppressive. On
his authority, the church defended the legitimacy of male
rule, slavery, and Christian religious exclusivism.[2]

Male Rule

Several of the letters attributed to Paul appropriate the
structures and norms of the patriarchal culture in which
the early church took root. Women were instructed to be
subject to their husbands, submissive, and silent. The patriarchal household provided the model for the "household
of God" (Eph 2:19; 1 Tim 3:15). The primary value in
the hierarchical structure of the household—whether as the
empire itself or the individual patriarchal family—is obedience by subordinate members. All members have their designated place in the household. Masters have their place;
slaves have their place. Keeping one's place was paramount.
Later, male theologians joined their pagan counterparts
in blaming women for bringing evil into the world. They

deepened the inequality between male and female natures in the prevailing anthropology by asserting that only males possess the image of God.

Slavery

Until the late nineteenth century, the Catholic Church upheld the legitimacy of slavery as part of the order of creation. The Pauline texts provided the basis in revelation for the justification of the social institution of slavery. To revelation was added the reasoned arguments of Aristotle and Augustine. Writing in the fourth century B.C.E., the Greek philosopher Aristotle defined slavery as "natural." He argued that by nature some human beings are born to rule and others to be ruled, an argument he applied to gender subordination as well.

Augustine, the fifth-century C.E. Christian bishop of Hippo, supported the inequality of the patriarchal household. He argued that slavery—unlike gender domination—was "unnatural," a distortion of creation due to Adam's sin, but now a permanent punishment for original sin. Augustine developed a moral framework within which the relationship between master and slave could be evaluated.[3]

Christian Religious Exclusivism

In the Pauline letters theologians could find the elements of both an inclusionary and exclusionary theory of salvation. The assertion in 1 Timothy that God "desires everyone to be saved" grounded the inclusiveness of salvation (2:4). But this was accompanied by a further claim that restricted salvation to Christianity and seemed to nullify the salvific value of all other religions: "For there is one God; there is also one mediator between God and humankind, Christ Jesus, himself human, who gave himself a ransom for all—this was attested at the right time" (2:5–6).

In the tradition that followed, Christians focused particular attention on Judaism, arguing that Israel's covenant was null and void with the advent of Christ (Eph 2:15). Now the Gentiles, not the Jews, were God's elect (Titus 1:1).

Over the centuries, persistent religious hostility of Christians toward Jews generated violence against them in the social order. What started out in the first century as an intra-Jewish polemic became by the end of the century a Gentile polemic against the Jews and in the centuries to come a full-fledged bias that would be named anti-Semitism only in the modern era.

The effects of these understandings of Paul's letters have been tragic. For centuries Christian theologians defended hierarchy and domination as God's will for the created order. Some still do. But at least today we have those who help us see domination from the perspective of the victim. Domination is not a birthright of some but an acquired sin, a systemic ideology of superiority—race, gender, class—that constitutes the sin of the world. Insofar as religious meaning justifies domination, it contributes to the alienation of humankind from God.

LITERARY JUDGMENTS

For Paul's voice to authorize these three positions radically marginalizes his moral significance. How can his worldview be a moral source for Christians if it incorporates immoral positions within it? This matter of problematic texts received as revelation presents a dilemma. But the moral question should be set aside until a literary one has been addressed first.

The literary question regards the authorship of all the letters ascribed to Paul. Even in the early church, questions were raised about the authorship of certain of the New Testament writings. In the second century, the theologian Origen had doubts about the letters of James and 2 Peter, concluding his inquiry into the matter with the remark, "Only God knows."[4] But it was not until the nineteenth century that authorship of individual Pauline letters was questioned. Did Paul write Colossians, Ephesians, and 1 Timothy? To put it more directly: Did Paul write the letters that authorize slavery and male rule? Differences in language, style, and theological perspective have led scholars to designate six of the letters as inauthentic, attributed to Paul but not written by him, and seven as authentic, attributed to and in fact written by him. The image of the church as the household of God and the justification of male and class privilege appear in the inauthentic letters. Paul did not authorize slavery or male rule.

We will refer to the Paul of the authentic or undisputed letters as the "historical Paul" and the Paul of the disputed letters as the "attributed Paul." The writer or writers of the disputed letters remain anonymous. But once we know which letters belong to whom, they can be compared. The attributed Paul differs from the historical Paul on the nature of the *ekklēsia*—assembly—of believers, the participation of female and male members in the assembly, and the criteria for full membership. The attributed Paul has dominated the tradition. The writers assumed Paul's authority to present views that were very different than his own.

With regard to religious privilege in particular, there is yet a third Paul, the Paul of the *adversus Judaeos* tradition. This is the Paul who announced God's rejection of the Jews. This Paul is boldly supersessionist, dismissing the salvific value of all religious traditions except Christianity. In the twentieth century it was the historical disregard of the Jews by Christians that allowed Adolf Hitler to undertake genocide against them. Changing the way Christians think and talk about Jews and Judaism and the way in which the relation between Judaism and Christianity is conceived has become a crucial theological task.[5]

DISCOVERING PAUL

In the work ahead, we want to discover the Paul deeply committed to the God of Israel and embarked on a passionate journey of faith. His journey and passion, though, must be disentangled from the Paul portrayed as disdaining Jewish law and rejecting Judaism altogether. Paul inspires us to be transformed by the experience of belonging to Christ as was the historical Paul. But belonging need not be religiously exclusive, dismissing the salvific value of other traditions. Nor should it authorize hierarchy and relations of domination as did the attributed Paul. In our use and appreciation of Paul we must separate these other voices that have spoken in his name.

Paul's influence on the church has been profound, but over the centuries many victims could have testified that his words were used to reinforce their subjugation and to support the interests of the powerful. I believe that, once separated from those who have spoken for him, a Paul firmly committed to freedom and human flourishing can be discovered. He is not perfect, but in an evolutionary world such as our own the ideal is no longer perfection but becoming and authenticity. Differently, but no less than to his own assemblies, Paul can speak to our time and place. The Come & See series offers us a chance to engage ethical and evaluative questions that often do not find their way into an introduction to Paul. Without them so much can be misunderstood. With the help of the work of many wonderful Pauline scholars, we can encounter the authentic Paul through the letters received and cherished in the early church.

WITH APPRECIATION

In a teaching career that now extends over a number of years, several cities, and several universities, I have been fortunate to teach the New Testament and to deal with the letters of Paul on a regular basis. I am grateful to those who broke through stereotypes from the past to establish not simply the Jewishness of Paul and the Jesus movement as an extrinsic designation but as the intrinsic and defining feature of the worldviews of both the man and the movement. The first fruit of this engagement was my book *Paul and the Gentile Women*. When the conflict in Galatians is shown to be about membership, the question of gender is spontaneous, or at least can be, if we do not equate Gentiles or Galatians with "those that will be circumcised." What were the implications of the circumcision preaching for women in the Galatian communities? *Paul and the Gentile Women* develops an argument in response to this question. I am honored that Sigueme Publishers included this book in their monograph series, Estudios Biblicos Minor. The Spanish title is *Pablo de Tarso y las primeras christianas gentiles.*

I dealt with Paul through the historical lens of empire in "Paul and Early Christianity," in *Empire and the Christian Tradition: New Readings of Classical Theologians,* edited by Kwok Pui Lan, Don H. Compier, and Joerg Rieger. The present book, *Encountering Paul,* originated with an invitation from Jeremy Langford, formerly the editorial director of Sheed & Ward. I appreciate the reinforcement of this invitation to contribute to the Come & See series by Sarah Stanton, the present editor, and for her encouragement in its completion.

Along the way to completion, friends and family have read the manuscript of *Encountering Paul.* I would like to thank Beverly Schmitt, Madeline Boucher, and my children, Rachel West and Nathan West, for their time and work in looking it over. I am deeply grateful for the generosity of time and insight that my husband, Michael West, gives to my work.

Paul's World

To a resident of the first-century city of Jerusalem who knew of the Jesus movement, Jesus' brother, James, would have appeared the most influential of Jesus followers. And if not James, then Jesus' disciples Peter and John might have come to notice. Perhaps a woman disciple in Jesus' inner circle, Mary Magdalene, would have been the subject of conversation.

But it is surprising to find that Paul, who figures so prominently in the New Testament and tradition, would have drawn little attention at the time. The fact that his ministry was in the Diaspora, that is, among Jews outside Judea, accounts for his invisibility in Jerusalem. Paul was not part of Jesus' inner circle; in fact, he had not even known Jesus or followed him during his ministry.

From our vantage point centuries later, things are reversed. It is Paul who overshadows the Jerusalem disciples completely. Many today do not even know that Jesus had a brother who played a significant role in the movement beginning after the experience of the risen Jesus. Only with modern biblical scholarship have we understood how the marginalization of James occurred historically. John Painter calls attention to the way in which the writer of the Acts of the Apostles—commonly thought to be the same as the writer of the Gospel of Luke—treats James. James's name tells us something about him. Known as "James the Just" or "James the Righteous," his name pointed to his continued fidelity to the way of living mandated for Jews by the Torah. Painter argues that Luke "sought to minimize the role of James because he was aware that James represented a hard-line position on the place of circumcision and the keeping of the law, a position that Luke himself did not wish to retain."[1] Luke relegated James to a walk-on part and elevated Paul from the margins to center stage. Even the major city shifted. Jerusalem moved offstage, and Rome assumed a prominence that endures to the present time.

We know Paul through the letters that were preserved and included in the New Testament canon. Theologians and biblical scholars have spent much time and effort in trying to discern the core of Paul's theology. What is the one idea around which everything else revolves? What captures the very essence of his theological perspective? Today this interest has changed. It is not the one big concept but the context that scholars seek. How do we understand Paul in the social and historical context of his time? What did he think of the empire whose standing army was a constant reminder of the violence that would ensue at the slightest infraction on Israel's part? Where did he fit in the diversity of parties in Second Temple Judaism? What were the communities like that he founded? Paul's theology was not principally shaped by concepts—although certainly by Israel's symbols of election and covenant—but by these multiple contexts that made up his social world. They will be our starting point.[2]

SECOND TEMPLE JUDAISM

To conceive of Judaism as a religion—separate from politics or economics, for example—in first-century Palestine is anachronistic. Religion for us in the modern world, at least in the United States, is separated constitutionally from the political realm. But in the ancient world religion was embedded in the other major institutions of the social order. Political commitments were expressed in religious rituals and so forth. Judaism was not a part of the social order but the people of Israel themselves, a nation, a distinct ethnic group, a sociopolitical and economic entity. The Torah, odd as it sounds, was their national constitution. Granted, it is a religious document, but one in which religion, family, politics, and economics are interwoven and not separate institutions.

The singular *Judaism* is anachronistic as well.[3] After the destruction of the Temple in 70 C.E., Jewish religious life became centered in the synagogue with the rabbi as leader and teacher. But in the first part of the century, during the lives of Jesus and Paul, Judaism is better seen as "Judaisms." Jews were diverse in their interpretations of themselves. Different parties or groups were active and contentious in the first century. Each understood Israel's main symbols—land, election, covenant—differently. They vied with one another for followers, for privileges, for dominance politically. They purposely divided up as classes, and by virtue of the kind of roles they played in Jewish life. For all, however, the Temple played a central role in their self-understanding.

Scholars use the term *Second Temple Judaism* as a neutral description of the period of Jewish history from the return from exile in the sixth century B.C.E. to the destruction of the rebuilt Second Temple in 70 C.E. It replaces terms such as *late Judaism* with which Christians implied that the end of Judaism was near with the advent of Christianity. This and other terms which imply that Christianity replaced Judaism are part of a theological worldview called supersessionism. Supersessionist theology is negative and polemical. We have learned only recently that the supersessionist portrayal of Judaism and Jews does not correspond with historical reality.

JEWISH DIVERSITY

What Jewish groups were prominent in the first century? How did they correspond to classes and interest groups? Paul's world was one in which different groups competed with one another for allegiance. Surely some groups active then are lost to history. But some became part of the historical memory. We know something about the following groups.

Sadducees

The Sadducees were linked with the Jewish aristocracy or elite class. Wealth often came from large landholdings, a result more often than not of the misfortunes of those who fell into debt and lost their land as a consequence. In ancient Israel the priesthood was inherited, and priestly families in the Sadducees controlled the Temple. Interests in maintaining wealth and privilege led this group to collaborate with Roman occupiers, a major reason for the poor and less privileged to dislike them.

Essenes

The Essenes were religious Jews who withdrew from Jewish society, largely because they thought the priestly families were corrupt and their control of the Temple a defamation. A priestly sect, they formed a monastic community. The Essenes are identified with the community at Qumran that produced the scrolls archaeologists found in caves on the northwest side of the Dead Sea in 1945, now referred to as the Dead Sea Scrolls.

Zealots

The Zealots were revolutionary Jews intent on freeing Israel from the political occupation the Romans had established in 63 B.C.E. They were responsible for several attempts to overthrow Roman rule, including the revolt in 66 C.E. and the ensuing Jewish-Roman War that ended in 70 C.E. with the Romans' destruction of the Temple and the city of Jerusalem. Jesus is not thought to be associated with the Zealots, but his use of the Jewish symbol of *basileia tou theou*—Empire of God—mediated a not-so-subtle critique of the Empire of Rome. The values underlying God's empire and Rome's empire are quite different.

Pharisees

Pharisees figure in the Gospel narratives and the story of Jesus as well as the life of Paul. They originated as a reform movement and by the first century they had been active as a party for two centuries. They were laymen committed to a lifestyle that placed covenant fidelity and following the Torah at the heart of life. Appropriating the standards of purity designated for priests, men identified with Pharisaic Judaism tried to live all of life "as if one were in the Temple." They wanted to make ordinary life holy by heightened attention to the rituals and practices the Torah demanded of them. This lifestyle set them apart from others. Like the Essenes, the Pharisees were opposed to what they considered to be the corruption of the priestly families. But unlike the Essenes, they did not withdraw from the social world.

Because they focused on the written Torah as the means of covenant fidelity, the Pharisees studied the law carefully. To live it, one had to know it well. Consequently, they became known as scholars of the law. Acts 22:3 portrays Paul as a student in Jerusalem with a leading Pharisaic rabbi, Gamaliel. Some biblical scholars believe this attribution tells us more about the writer of Acts than about Paul. The writer of Acts may have wanted to identify Paul with the liberal wing of the Pharisaic party with which Gamaliel was associated. He is described as having argued before the Sanhedrin for toleration of the Jewish messianic movement that began after Jesus' death (5:33–39). The Sanhedrin was the supreme judicial and administrative council responsible for handling the affairs of Jews in Palestine.

The New Testament writers portray the Pharisees negatively. This is a polemical portrayal of them, not an accurate historical portrayal. It reflects the later intra-Jewish conflict between messianic Jews who proclaimed that God's raising Jesus from the dead had validated him as God's mediator of salvation and Jews who rejected this claim about a crucified man. In the Gospel of Matthew, for instance the portrayal of conflict between the Pharisees and Jesus reflects more the conflict between Pharisees and members of Matthew's community rather than that of Jesus. Decades after Jesus' death, it was Matthew's community who was in competition with the Pharisees for leadership of Israel after the failure of the Jewish revolt against Rome. The Pharisaic party became influential in shaping Rabbinic Judaism and replacing the Temple cult with the centrality of synagogue and prayer.

That separation between Rabbinic Judaism and Christianity occurred in the second century, well after Paul's time in the 50s and 60s of the first century. His proclamation of the risen Christ takes place in the context of the people of Israel.

Messianic Jews

Along with the Sadducees, Essenes, and Zealots, the Messianic Jews—Jesus followers—added their voice proclaiming God's validation of the crucified Jesus. Their interpretation of Jesus' death reflects the centrality of the Temple in their religious worldview and an understanding of sacrifice as a means of reconciliation of humankind with God.

THE PEOPLE OF ISRAEL

By the time of Jesus and Paul, Israel had experienced more than a 1,000-year history, beginning with the call of Abraham and Sarah, through the time of the tribal confederacy, monarchy, divided kingdoms, exile, and then later foreign occupation by Rome.[4]

Election

Over those long centuries, at the heart of the self-understanding of the people of Israel stood the conviction that Yahweh, the God of Israel, had chosen Israel as a special people. This symbol of election shapes the perspective especially of the Book of Deuteronomy. Election came with a purpose. By Israel's example, "all nations" would come to the worship of the true God. This idea that Israel's covenant would someday be open to Gentiles defines Paul's ministry. In terms of Israel's election, the biblical writers emphasize that God's choice of them was due to God's love, not to their merit. As the Deuteronomist puts it, "do not say to yourself, 'It was because of my righteousness.'" Their election was owed to the divine initiative and to love:

> It was not because you were more numerous than any other people that the LORD set his heart on you and chose you—for you were the fewest of all peoples. It was because the LORD loved you and kept the oath that he swore to your ancestors, that the LORD has brought you out with a mighty hand, and redeemed you from the house of slavery, from the hand of Pharaoh king of Egypt. (Deut 7:7–8)

Temple

For all the differences among the Judaisms, they were one in the centrality of the Jerusalem Temple. The Temple was conceived to be Yahweh's earthly dwelling place. But it was not only a sacred space for worship. The Temple was an economic, political, and civic center for Jews. The Temple that Jesus and Paul attended was actually the third Temple. Solomon's Temple was destroyed by the Babylonians in their conquest of Judea in 586 B.C.E. Those who returned from exile some fifty years later began rebuilding it. This Second Temple was dedicated about 515 B.C.E. (As noted, scholars refer to the time between the Babylonian conquest in the sixth century B.C.E. and Roman destruction of Jerusalem in 70 C.E. as the Second Temple Period.) The magnificent reconstruction of this Second Temple undertaken by Herod the Great is considered a third Temple. It was this Temple that the Romans destroyed in 70 C.E., about six years after the death of Paul.

Land

The biblical traditions carried God's promise of the land of Canaan to Abraham and his descendants (Gen 15:7, 18). Canaan was located between Syria and Egypt. The liberation of the Hebrews from the slavery they came to endure in Egypt and the beginning of their journey back to Canaan is the story of the Exodus (Exod 1–15). The books of Joshua and Judges continue that story and their settlement in Canaan. The land was divided into two kingdoms after the reign of Solomon in the tenth century

B.C.E. The northern kingdom was called Israel and the southern kingdom Judea. Jerusalem was the capital city of Judea. At the time of Jesus and Paul, the Romans referred to the regions of Judea, Galilee, and Samaria as Palestine. The names by which this ethic group were known also have a history. The earliest term is *Hebrews*. The term *Jew*, for "Judah-ite" (Hebrew *yehudi*), was given to those returning from the Babylonian Exile in 537 B.C.E. Some scholars consider *Judeans* the correct designation for the ethnic group in the first century. *Jew* became the Greco-Roman name for inhabitants of Judea but was not the preferred self-designation of the people. Their preferred term was *Yisra'el*, Israel, and *B'nei Yisra'el* or children or people of Israel. It is common today to use the term *Israelite* for the people of the Hebrew Bible and *Jew* for persons since the first century C.E.

Covenant

The traditions of Israel depict Yahweh entering into a relationship of fidelity with Noah (Gen 6:18), with Abraham (Gen 17:10), and with Moses. It is this last covenant at Mount Sinai (Exod 19:1) that constitutes the people as Israel. In the ancient world a covenant was a political agreement between two parties of unequal power. There were obligations and responsibilities on both sides. When a more powerful king, for example, entered into a covenant with a less powerful king, promising protection on his part, the subordinate king promised loyalty and tribute. Israel appropriated the notion of covenant to portray a relationship between the human and divine.

Here, as in the political realm, there were promises and obligations on both sides. Yahweh's promise was that Israel would be "my treasured people out of all the peoples." Israel's obligation was to "obey my voice and keep my covenant" (Exod 19:5). A covenant-making ceremony is found in Deuteronomy 26:16–19. "Today you have obtained the LORD's agreement: to be your God" (26:17). The metaphor "obey my voice" directed Israel to do God's will. The prophet Amos put God's will in its most basic ethical form: "Seek good and not evil, that you may live; and so the LORD, the God of hosts, will be with you, just as you have said. Hate evil and love good, and establish justice in the gate" (5:14–15).

Torah

The written Torah is constituted by the first five books of the Hebrew Bible. It is also called the Pentateuch. Torah is often translated "law," but a more accurate translation for its meaning is "way of living." The phrase *works of the law* is shorthand for "living as a Jew." The dominant perspective of the Torah is that of the priests who brought Israel's traditions together into the written form they have now. The priestly editing of the Torah took place during the Babylonian Exile in the sixth-century B.C.E. As the priestly writers present it, Israel's covenant obligation was to do God's will and to be like God, "to be a people holy to the LORD your God" (Deut 26:18–19). The Torah itself was understood to be God's gift of the means to fulfill this obligation. It constituted a way of living, applying to all of life, not just to a separate religious realm. It provided the norm for the meaning of righteousness and sin, that is, to right and wrong relation to God. The Torah-observant person is in right relation to God (righteous). The nonobservant person or the person in violation of the Torah is in the wrong relation to God (sinner). While Jews debated the status of Gentiles in relation to the law, just the fact that they were nonobservant made them sinners by default.

The Torah is replete with references to the relation between obedience to the law and Israel's possession of the land and well-being. Possession was contingent on obedience:

> You must follow exactly the path that the LORD your God has commanded you, so that you may live, and that it may go well with you, and that you may live long in the land you are to possess. (Deut 5:33)

Moses reminds the people:

> Take care that you do not forget the LORD your God, by failing to keep his commandments, his ordinances, and his statutes, which I am commanding you today. (Deut 8:11)

ROMAN EMPIRE

The Jewish world of Palestine and the Diaspora—in fact, what was considered the known world—was dominated by the Roman Empire. Roman control originated with and was sustained with violence. Rome's standing armies kept subject peoples subdued, and its exploitative economic system kept people poor or, if elite and wealthy, kept them in collaboration with the oppressors. Its oppressive politics trumped the rule of law as well as revolutionary attempts to restore independence.

Walter Wink describes an empire as a domination system.[5] It is characterized by rigid class stratification and a great disparity in wealth between the elite and nonelite. Empires operate on exclusions and inequities rather than inclusion and equality. Usually subject people are drawn into the empire, losing their social, economic, and political autonomy. In contrast, Jews were granted some rights by the Romans—they could worship their own God and were exempt from the obligation to participate in the imperial cult. They could observe their own religious customs, and they could gather in synagogues. They were allowed a Jewish king, an ambiguous privilege given the murderous tendencies of a ruler such as Herod the Great. But disturbances could bring a Roman prefect or governor to enforce Roman rule directly. Such was the position of Pontius Pilate, the Roman official who sent Jesus to his death.

Jewish parties disagreed on the levels of conformity or resistance to Roman rule that they should maintain. But if they were elite and wealthy, collaboration was the only way to retain their lifestyle. Most people did not have wealth to protect, and they undertook various strategies of resistance: anticolonial actions. Dispossessed peasants resisted increased taxation and occupation by foreign troops through "social banditry." K. C. Hanson and Douglas Oakman write that social bandits "lash out by organizing into bands that raid and steal to survive, usually from the local and imperial elites."[6]

The Wisdom of Solomon is a response to Roman occupation. The writing condemns the violence of the Romans as well as the failure of the Jewish leaders to protect the Temple and the people. It expresses eschatological hope for God's justice to set the situation right. God will save Israel and punish both Gentile oppressors and Jewish elites for their sins of violence and theft against the people.[7]

STRATEGIES OF RESISTANCE

Both Jesus and Paul engaged in strategies of resistance. Both rejected the way of violence chosen by some and the collaboration chosen by others. Both utilized eschatological expectations and hopes as a means of resistance. God's *basileia*, or empire, functioned as both contrast to and critique of Rome's *basileia*. By evoking God's empire Jesus held up an alternative to the existing empire. The contrast contained an implicit challenge: the beginning of empire implies the end of the other. Pontius Pilate's crucifixion of Jesus under the title "King of the Jews" was likely meant to ridicule the possibility of challenge to the empire.

Paul's proclamation of the risen Christ undermined the ultimate claims that the empire made for itself. Today we may easily miss the challenge and offense given by preaching the crucified Christ within the empire that crucified him. In effect Paul was saying that Caesar's power had been usurped by an itinerant Jewish preacher. The one who died powerless against the empire was now proclaimed Lord of all.

An even more direct challenge to the empire is offered in the images of Christ's return and judgment. Paul's language of Christ's return is extremely abrasive:

> Then comes the end, when he hands over the kingdom to God
> the Father, after he has destroyed every ruler and every author-
> ity and power. For he must reign until he puts all his enemies
> under his feet. (1 Cor 15:24–25)

Because eschatological expectations are of future events, some Jews and Christians looked to various events to signal the beginning of the end time. The end was uniformly considered to be twofold: first, an act of divine judgment rendering punishment to the wicked and vindication to the righteous; and second, the establishment of God's rule. Among various signals, resurrection of the dead was one kind of event thought to open history to its eschatological fulfillment. The Jesus followers' proclamation of the risen Jesus did not convince Paul initially, but after his personal mystical experience in which "God . . . was pleased to reveal his Son to me" (Gal 1:15–16), Paul never deviated from his conviction that the eschatological age had dawned and that divine judgment was close at hand. Now was the time for repentance.

Believers waited for God to send his Son from heaven who "rescues us from the wrath that is coming" (1 Thess 1:10). Evoking explicitly military images, Paul says of Christ's coming, "For the Lord himself, with a cry of command, with the archangel's call and with the sound of God's trumpet, will descend from heaven, and the dead in Christ will rise first" (1 Thess 4:16).

Exempting the assembly from those on whom sudden destruction will come, Paul writes, "For God has destined us not for wrath but for obtaining salvation through our Lord Jesus Christ" (1 Thess 5:9). In yet another letter

Paul contrasts the citizenship of the believers with others: "Their end is their destruction; their god is the belly; and their glory is in their shame; their minds are set on earthly things" (Phil 3:19). Power is given to Christ "to make all things subject to himself" (Phil 3:21).

It is only the lack of historical consciousness and distance from the social context of the first century that allows us to miss this element. We do not identify explicitly with imperial and Roman leaders of Paul's time. When he describes every rule, every authority as belonging on the side of darkness and death, he is talking about actual persons. He had his fair share of emperors—and brutal tyrants—to choose from: Nero (54–68 C.E.), who was responsible for Paul's own death; Claudius (41–54 C.E.); and Caligula (37–41 C.E.), to name those during his missionary life.

PAX ROMANA

After the assassination of Julius Caesar, the dictator of the Roman Republic, in 44 B.C.E., civil war lasted for over a decade. In the end, Octavius Augustus, the adopted son of Julius Caesar, became the first emperor to rule what was then the Roman Empire. He considered the end to civil war—peace—his greatest achievement. The Pax Romana, as this period is called, lasted through several emperors from 27 B.C.E. to 180 C.E. *Pax Augustus* is written on some altars dedicated to Augustus. Without the constant need to attend to armies and battles, attention was turned to developing the things now identified as Rome's great accomplishments, such as their systems of roads, other civil works, and laws.

The perspective of those colonized by Rome reveals something different about this peace. Roman coins depict a male prisoner of war and a woman mourning. But the emperor's achievement was experienced, from below, as subjugation, with nation after nation violently added to the imperial territory. The Romans described the Pax Romana as "salvation," what saved nations from the bloodshed of ongoing war. But salvation seen from on top meant loss of freedom and independence, and subservience to Rome from the bottom.

Paul countered the Pax Romana with the peace of Christ. This peace is a cosmic one. Through the death of Christ, reconciliation with God is achieved for all. Paul makes a clear reference to the empire in his reference to "peace and security" in 1 Thessalonians 5:3. He predicts destruction:

> For you yourselves know very well that the day of the Lord will come like a thief in the night. When they say, "There is peace and security," then sudden destruction will come upon them, as labor pains come upon a pregnant woman, and there will be no escape! (1 Thess 5:2–3)

But the peace of Christ comes only after judgment. The "day of the Lord" will be a day of destruction for "them." "They" are the Romans whose description of this period of calm as "peace" is a lie. Their "peace and security" results from the murderous colonization of the Mediterranean world, the enslavement of people of numerous nations, and the plunder of the national treasure and natural resources of others.

The empire is a history of death that will not continue. The eschatological coming of Jesus will radically change the world. When it establishes God's *basileia*, Jesus' arrival will mean the end of Rome's *basileia*. The day of the Lord will spell deliverance for his followers. If it is liberation from "them," it is liberation from Rome (1 Thess 5:1–3). The image of this day is that of the destruction of imperial power and the unjust institutions that perpetuate it. In 1 Corinthians Paul makes an incredibly blunt statement: Christ will destroy every rule, power, authority (15:24). They belong on the side of darkness and death. There was at the time of Paul one rule, one power, one authority— Rome—and whatever subsidiary power was given to others by Rome. His statement is not abstract but concrete.

GOSPEL OF CAESAR

Christian appropriation of the imperial term for official messages of the emperor, *gospel*, is similar to that of Pax Romana. As an imperial message, the gospel of Caesar was a proclamation or announcement of good news for the emperor: the birth of a child, the ascension of a new king, and so forth. But the news may not be so good for the one receiving it. The emperor might proclaim with gladness a military victory over another nation, which the defeated would not hear as good news.

The Hebrew Bible anticipates good news of God's intervention on behalf of God's people. Eschatological expectations of God's reign express hope that this good news will be realized one day. The New Testament gospels, written after Paul, talk about the good news of Jesus. The good news is that God is for the poor and the marginalized and God's reign is near. This was not news that the imperial authorities welcomed.

An empire keeps its power by limiting the voices that can speak. It does not engage in an exchange of ideas. Those who threaten its authority in any way face its violence. Suspected insurrectionists were made into a public example for everyone. Crucifixion was a favored means of imperial political execution.[8] Preceded by beatings and torture, crucifixion inflicted the ultimate punishment on those who had threatened the established order. Naked, nailed to a cross, the victim suffered unspeakable pain and the degradation of a slow and public death. Jesus died such a death. For those who watched, the imperial message was clear: *this could be you.*[9]

In light of what was done to Jesus, Paul's integration of an early Christian hymn in his letter to the Philippians almost seems to invite such a fate for himself.[10] What ruler would not hear the description of Jesus and what is owed to him as a challenge to the emperor personally and to the political order?

> Therefore God also highly exalted him and gave him the name that is above every name, so that at the name of Jesus every knee should bend, in heaven and on earth and under the earth, and every tongue should confess that Jesus Christ is Lord, to the glory of God the Father. (Phil 2:9–11)

To claim that people should bend their knees to anyone other than the emperor is astounding enough. Imperial authorities and local ruling elites were known for their paranoia and the use of violence as a quick solution to perceived threats. But that knees would bend to a slave would have been insulting rather than astounding:

> Let the same mind be in you that was in Christ Jesus, who, though he was in the form of God did not regard equality with God as something to be exploited, but emptied himself, taking the form of a slave; being born in human likeness. (Phil 2:5–7)

This hymn is pre-Pauline. Paul did not write it; he used it. It reflects a community whose Jesus tradition is one of exaltation rather than resurrection. There is no resurrection in this passage. The hymn reflects the consciousness of a group who see through the false values of their culture, from the bottom up, so to speak. The hymn takes the chief value of Roman culture, honor, and portrays the crucified Jesus—one who dies without honor—as validated "beyond measure" by God's exaltation of him. Jesus is "obedient to the point of death, death on a cross" (2:8), then exalted by God. The hymn further inverts the cultural competition for honor by identifying Jesus with a slave, one whose honor is so nonexistent that he or she is denied even the status of person.

The Romans celebrated their military victories by returning with thousands of slaves from conquered territories and parading them through the city. For the ordinary person, the roads to slavery were multiple: pirates scooped up families and villages, military battles took whole regions, and exorbitant taxes created such debt as to throw virtually any peasant into slavery. The world of Jesus and Paul was a slave state. At some later point, the imbalance between slave and free even threatened the existence of the empire itself.

Honor is a limited good in this world. For one's honor to increase requires a decrease in honor for another. Slavery could be said to be a vital negative in such a culture. This "social death," as Orlando Patterson calls it, means that honor for some rises dramatically.[11]

The link between obedience and death in the Philippians' hymn reverses the situation brought about by Adam's sin. Adam's disobedience brought death. Jesus' obedience took him through death to new life as Lord. So "Jesus Christ is Lord" is a transcendent claim. It means that as Lord, Jesus possesses all in his domain. "Heaven, earth and under the earth" signal that his domain is everything. The emperor's claim to possess the world is subverted by the even greater claim that Christ possesses the universe.

Among Jesus followers, the confession, "Our Lord, Come!" (1 Cor 16:22) was a transliteration of Aramaic *maranatha*. Pre-Pauline in origin, acclamations like these come from early Christian worship. Paul uses "Jesus is Lord" twenty-four times in his first letter to the Thessalonians, even as he is talking about the persecution they may have suffered for doing so themselves (1 Thess 1:6). In the first chapter alone of 1 Corinthians he uses some variation of it fifteen times. It designates the unequaled status given to Jesus by God. In the words of Larry Hurtado, this Jesus devotion was "a striking innovation."[12]

Paul's language for Christ draws from and decenters the imperial cult. The Roman religion with its goddesses and gods—Jupiter, Mars, Diana, Juno, Minerva, Apollo—was fused in the first century with the worship of the emperor. Julius Caesar's claim to be a descendant of Aeneas, the legendary founder of Rome and son of Venus, the goddess of love and beauty, laid the groundwork for this imperial inflation. Octavian, his adopted son, claimed that the flash of Halley's Comet was the spirit of Caesar entering heaven. With Caesar a god, Octavian—then known as Augustus—claimed for himself the title Son of God, as did subsequent emperors. As the imperial cult became fused with Roman religious practices, offering sacrifices to the emperor became common. As emperor of Rome, Augustus was *Pontifex Maximus*, the highest priest of Roman religion. The Senate proclaimed Augustus a god at his death.

Paul appropriated these imperial titles to the risen Christ. He is Lord. He is Son of God (Gal 2:20). Inasmuch as a son receives legitimacy from the status of his father, Jesus' lineage trumps that of Julius Caesar and Aeneas. The reign Jesus initiates is without the violence of the existing empire. In identifying with the lowest of low, as the Philippians' hymn shows, the cosmic rule of Jesus is to be very different from that of the present rulers.

PAUL'S DEATH

Paul was likely killed in Rome as part of the persecution of Nero, emperor from 54 to 68 C.E. It is not known exactly when or how. According to the third-century theologian Tertullian, Paul was beheaded. The evidence for determining the manner of his death is lacking. But that imperial powers killed Paul would not be surprising. What is sur-

prising is the length of his ministry, which was allowed to
continue some thirty years.

QUESTIONS FOR
REFLECTION AND DISCUSSION

1. Name several ways in which first-century Judaism
   was diverse.
2. How was Jesus' preaching a strategy of resistance to
   the Roman Empire?
3. What is political in Paul's proclamation of Jesus that
   is often missed?

Expectations and Hopes

Because creation is an expression of divine creativity, the biblical writers affirm that it is good. Yet the goodness that creation derives from its transcendent source is thoroughly distorted by evil. More than individual acts, the Bible observes, violence, domination, and privilege skew the social institutions of family, law, economics, politics, and religion. The very institutions created to serve the common good cater instead to individual and group interests. The historical situation is a reversal of what God intends for the created order. The biblical image of the "reign of evil" conveys the pervasiveness of this distortion.

The related biblical hope that God would act in the future on behalf of Israel was deeply embedded in the religious worldview of Second Temple Judaism.[1] Israel's subjugation to a foreign power, the ever-present threat of standing armies, and crushing taxation were evils faced every day. Foreign oppression was made even more insidious by the collaboration of the native elites. Imposition of foreign practices and the restriction of freedom to observe native customs supplied key conditions for messianic movements.

Eschatological hopes and expectations shaped the horizon of Second Temple Judaism. Pharisaic Judaism and messianic Judaism shared the apocalyptic images of a future wrath and judgment, a new covenant, and Gentiles coming to worship the true God of Israel. Paul's allegiance shifted from one group to the other. This change did not introduce new expectations but instead quickened his sense of their relation to the present and future. With the risen Jesus, future expectations were being realized in the present. "Now is the day of salvation," Paul wrote to the Corinthians (2 Cor 2:2). In this chapter we explore the worldview engendered for Jesus, his followers, and Paul by these expectations and hopes.

JEWISH RESTORATION ESCHATOLOGY

Scholars refer to this complex set of images and ideas as Jewish restoration eschatology. It deals with the complexity or layers of unintelligibility that evil introduces into historical process, not in a systematic fashion but in pictures, so to speak. "Wrath," "judgment," and "evildoers" evoke images. This kind of thinking portrays the historical situation as a drama. "Wrath" and "judgment" will punish the "evildoers" and vindicate the "righteous." The identity of the evildoers, the righteous, and the judge is known to the insiders for whom the apocalyptic language serves as a code to talk about social and political realities.

Eschaton means end time. But as we have suggested already, "end" does not mean the end of history itself but rather the end of a stage of history. It is a decisive time: God is going to do something. A new reign implies the end of the present reign. The reign of evil—the present reign—is one of injustice, inequality, and oppression. People are divided by such factors as class and gender into separate and unequal spheres. The new age will be one of ever-unfolding justice, equality, and inclusion. In the reign of God, compassion will replace violence.

Gerd Theissen and Annette Merz write that the expectation of God's rule or reign is grounded in the Jewish conception of God's "unconditional will for the good."[2] This rule is the establishment of God's ethical will, active in the present and future. It evokes a demand on the human ethical will. An announcement of both salvation and judgment, it has social and political, as well as personal, relevance. God's rule stands in contradiction to the existing rule.

Eschatological expectations and hopes are found in a Jewish literary genre called apocalypse from the Greek *apokalpsis*, meaning revelation or disclosure.[3] The terms *apocalyptic* and *eschatological* are used interchangeably to describe the thinking and language of this genre. Apocalyptic writings occur with some frequency in the three centuries before the Common Era. The Book of Revelation is a New Testament example of this genre. Many of them, pseudonymously or anonymously inscribed and not appearing in the official biblical canon, are called *pseudepigrapha*. The political dimension of apocalyptic literature is more appreciated today than before.

JESUS

Jesus announced the inbreaking of God's *basileia*.[4] This apocalyptic symbol, contrasting the reign of evil with the reign of God, would have been quite familiar to his audience. The symbol of *basileia* expressed hope that a social order distorted by evil would be set right by God's intervention. Chief among the factors that would set it right is liberation from foreign powers. Domination drives both patriarchy as a social system and empire as a political reality. God's *basileia* is domination-free.

In English, the terms *kingdom*, *reign*, or *rule* commonly translate *basileia*. However, Rome's use of the term is instructive. It was used by Rome for its imperial territories. *Basileia* means empire. With this translation in mind, what Jesus was up to becomes clearer. A contrast between empires is a method of critique. For Jesus to evoke God's *basileia* would have spontaneously created a contrast between the empire that was and the empire that could be.

The empire of Rome coincided with what Paul referred to as this present evil age. Its claim to power was absolute. Excessive violence was a key tool to keeping its claim effective. Jesus' preaching was a subtle but clear rejection of Rome's values. He did not seek what mattered so much to elites—honor, greatness, power. He embodied the values of God's *basileia* in his compassionate response to the exploited and marginalized. The good news he offered them was that God was for them, not for those whose privilege set them apart.

It has not been common in the Christian tradition to talk about the "economics of Jesus." But Jesus' audience would not have heard his preaching as somehow spiritual or religious, as opposed to economic or political. He prayed for the economic realities experienced by the oppressed to be changed: his praying for food implies a situation of hunger. Praying for work implies a situation of joblessness. Praying for shelter implies a situation of homelessness.

Jesus' contrast of empires evokes two very different ways of doing things in a social order and the values that generate those ways. The transformation of one way to another requires a reversal of values, a withdrawal first from the false values that generate social, political, economic, and religious inequities. It is then an appropriation of genuine values—equality, inclusion, justice. Unjust economic orders restrict the benefits of society to a few. Just economic orders generate political and economic strategies in which social benefits can be extended to all.

The social and political referent of Jesus' preaching has not always been appreciated. "The gospel is not a message of personal salvation from the world," Walter Wink writes, "but a message of a world transfigured, right down to its basic structures."[5] The symbol of God's *basileia* not only evoked an alternative to the present social order. Jesus' words, relationships, and actions embodied the *basileia*. In contrast to the violence and exploitation of Rome's empire, Jesus signaled the features of a domination-free order—equality, mutual respect, and partnership.[6] Their opposites—inequality, dehumanization, and oppression—characterize sin.

PAUL

Like Jesus, Paul's theological worldview included the eschatological horizon he shared with his contemporaries. Paul does not mention Jesus' preaching explicitly in his letters, but they share an eschatological horizon. The equality and inclusion promoted by Galatians 3:28 is the same transformation of the world envisioned by Jesus and announced in the images and words of his ministry.

For Jesus and Paul, God's reign was beginning. Paul perceived himself and his Gentile converts living in the in-between, between the initiation of the end time and the future judgment, when Christ as God's agent will return to punish the evil and vindicate the righteous. The present is a time of repentance and of holiness. Getting the Gentile men and women in his communities to work at the latter— to live ethical lives—and to keep them on the side of the righteous when Christ returned was one of Paul's major challenges. Paul could not draw explicitly on the Torah for moral guidance. His foundation for moral living was the Spirit of Christ. Lives of holiness and justice are empowered by the indwelling of the divine presence. In his appeal to the Corinthian women and men not to sin, he asks very simply, "Do you not realize that Jesus Christ is in you?" (2 Cor 13:5).

Once God had revealed the risen Christ to him, Paul took the resurrection event as the signal that the end time had come. By the "end," he did not envision the total annihilation of history as do modern fundamentalists, but rather the end of history dominated by evil. By raising one who had been killed by an empire that thought its power extended into the grave, God unmasked the illusion that lay under this conception of human power.

For those who suffer from the power and violence of others, eschatological expectation is hope that God will not let injustice go unchecked forever. It is the spontaneous sense, too, that the enormity of the problem caused by evil is beyond human beings to rectify. The solution is God's.

Paul portrays the scope of the problem by way of repeated lists of sins (Rom 1:28–31) and references to humankind's "ungodliness and wickedness" (Rom 1:18). He admonishes the Corinthians, saying, "I fear that there may perhaps be quarreling, jealousy, anger, selfishness, slander, gossip, conceit, and disorder. . . . I may have to mourn over many who previously sinned and have not repented of the impurity, sexual immorality, and licentiousness that they practiced" (2 Cor 12:20–21).

But sin is not all about sex. Imperial claims to absolute power are a significant dimension of the reign of evil. One wonders at Paul's nerve to announce that Christ will destroy "every ruler and every authority and power" (1 Cor 15:24–25). Eventually the imperial powers will end Paul's life as they did that of Jesus.

But death was not the last word. Paul remained convinced from the beginning of his ministry to the end that if he shared in the suffering and death of Christ, if he became "like him in his death," he would "attain the resurrection of the dead" (Phil 3:11). The believer can expect to share Christ's resurrection. In Romans, Paul stresses the consequence of being united with Christ: "For if we have been united with him in a death like his, we will certainly be united with him in a resurrection like his" (Rom 6:5). Or as he rephrases it: "But if we have died with Christ, we believe that we will also live with him" (Rom 6:7).

Some interpreters have tried to make the union with Christ in Romans 6:5 a kind of ontological incorporation that occurs in baptism or have argued that with Christ an objective change has occurred in the universe or human nature ending the reign of sin. David Brondos notes, however, that what Paul and believers in the Roman assembly understood was that "those who were baptized identified themselves as members of the people living under Christ who would inherit through him the life of the new age."[7] Brondos says that Paul is reminding people of what they already knew, "namely, that when they were baptized into the community of those believing in and following Christ, they made a radical break with the 'present evil age' characterized by sin and disobedience so as to identify fully with the age to come through Jesus."[8]

ESCHATOLOGICAL SYMBOLS

As a Pharisee and prior to his joining a messianic movement, Paul would have thought of resurrection and baptism in apocalyptic terms. In the context of Jewish restoration eschatology the event of resurrection was to signal that the end time had arrived and that God was beginning to act against evil. It pointed ahead to divine judgment. Judgment would separate the evil from the righteous, the former to be punished and the latter to be vindicated. The demand for now was for repentance and aligning oneself with the righteous.

Baptism, too, was an apocalyptic symbol. As Richard Horsley and Neil Silberman write, the practice of immersion was a powerful symbol in first-century Jewish life. It was seen as a metaphor for moral purification.[9] They cite a Hebrew prophet:

> Wash yourselves; make yourselves clean; remove the evil of your doings from before my eyes; cease to do evil; learn to do good; seek justice, rescue the oppressed, defend the orphan, plead for the widow. (Isaiah 1:16–17)

In the separatist Jewish monastic community at Qumran, declaring community membership and immersion signified that "the bather had rejected the entire complex of economics, political institutions, and cultural expression that was being carried on in mainstream society." John the Baptist made immersion available to all in his preaching of the coming of the day of judgment (Mark 1:4–5).

In the Pauline communities, too, undergoing baptism declared an individual's rejection of the values of the world—of a world divided by privilege and power—and acceptance of the values of the crucified Jesus raised by God. As a Pharisee, Paul would have seen observance of the law as the boundary marking covenant insider and outsider. Later, for Paul the apocalyptic Jew, Alan Segal writes, the eschatological symbol of baptism defined the boundary between outsider and insider.[10] In the patriarchal world in general and by the law specifically, women and men were divided into separate and unequal spheres. In the eschatological assembly, the original equality of women and men in creation was restored (Gen 1:27).

GENTILES

The biblical promise to Abraham was that all nations would come to the worship of the true God, the God of Israel, through him. This was an eschatological promise to be fulfilled in the end time. The purpose of Israel's election was not to be an isolated people but to bring all humankind to the prayer they called the Shema:

> Hear, O Israel: The LORD is our God, the LORD alone. You shall love the LORD your God with all your heart, and with all your soul, and with all your might. (Deut 6:4–5)

For Paul, the resurrection as an announcement that God was countering the distortion of evil and the inclusion of Gentiles into Israel's covenant were linked as eschatological images before his becoming a Jesus follower himself. His mission to the Gentiles makes sense in this context. Paul subsumes the historical Jesus into the risen Christ. Christ is present as Spirit; he will return as Lord in judgment. What was of ultimate significance about the historical Jesus was his death. Paul believed not only that by his death Jesus had atoned for Gentile sin but that it was the means by which God reconciled humanity to God's self and resurrection of Christ. With their debt paid and reconciliation having replaced alienation, Gentile women and men could now accept God's offer of salvation:

> They are now justified by his grace as a gift, through the redemption that is in Christ Jesus, whom God put forward as a sacrifice of atonement through his blood, effective through faith. (Rom 3:24)

The purpose of Paul's mission to the Gentiles followed the work of Christ:

> So if anyone is in Christ, there is a new creation: everything old has passed away; see, everything has become new! All this is from God, who reconciled us to himself through Christ, and has given us the ministry of reconciliation, that is, in Christ God was reconciling the world to himself; not counting their trespasses against them, and entrusting the message of reconciliation to us. (2 Cor 5:17–19)

Paul's position brought opposition from within the Jesus movement, to say nothing of Jews outside of the movement. At issue was the preservation of Jewish identity. The dominant view among Jews of the first century was that if Gentiles were to share the biblical promises given to Abraham, they would first become Jews. Even in the eschatological time, the boundary between covenant insider and outsider would remain.

But what Paul thought he was doing and what he was actually doing were two different matters. As E. P. Sanders writes, Paul understood himself as bringing Gentiles into the people of God, into Israel. He did not see his gospel as the break with Judaism that it was. This break, Sanders argues, is clearly perceptible at two points. "The first point is a denial of the election of Israel. The covenant for Paul now includes those in Christ, not Jews by descent. The second point is that Gentile women and men enter into the people of God through faith in Christ, not by accepting the law."[11]

Like the threat from the cultural influence of Hellenism, many Jews would have experienced Paul's gospel as a direct threat to the preservation of Jewish identity. That identity is clearly linked to a distinctive way of life. Proselytes shared in Israel's salvation by coming into Israel, by becoming Jewish, not, as Paul was preaching, by remaining as they were.[12]

DISCIPLESHIP COMMUNITY OF EQUALS

The assembly of believers is itself an eschatological symbol. The absence of privilege that creates a new social reality in the *ekklēsia* stands in contrast to the world. Their initiation into the community, like immersion at Qumran, expressed a fundamental change in worldview: "There is no longer Jew or Greek, there is no longer slave or master, there is no longer male and female; for you are all one in Christ Jesus" (Gal 3:28).

Hans Dieter Betz argues that the Gentile women and men who responded to Paul's preaching of "freedom in Christ" (Gal 5:1) understood this freedom as real.[13] They understood the eschatological assembly as an emancipatory one.

Elisabeth Schüssler Fiorenza writes, "In the new, Spirit-filled community of equals all distinctions of race, religion, class and gender are abolished. All are equal and one in Jesus Christ."[14] She describes the assembly as a "discipleship community of equals." While their language remained androcentric, Larry Hurtado reinforces the inclusion to which it pointed: "Galatians 3:28 makes it clear that female and male believers are included on an equal basis as 'sons' and 'heirs.'"[15] The indifference to gender in the ritual of initiation and in relations among members promoted the social integration of women in the Jesus assemblies.

The elimination of religious, ethnic, social, and gender oppositions in the *ekklēsia* is tied to the unity of Christ. They belong to Christ, are "in Christ," they are the body of Christ. The *ekklēsia* is an inclusive social reality, a new creation, in which both women and men stand in the same relation to God as "sons" (Gal 3:26) through their faith in Jesus Christ. Faith refers to the personal transformation each has undergone, in their experience of conversion and in the decision to turn away from idols and to the true God of Israel.

In the *ekklēsia*, participation and roles in ministry were shared by women and men. Romans 16 is an often-cited source for the names of women linked with different roles—apostle, evangelist, deacon. Throughout Paul's letters descriptions of roles are gender-neutral. James Dunn writes that "ministry in the Pauline churches belonged to all."[16]

Paul brought women and men into the eschatological Israel by way of religious conversion, the same way he himself had entered the messianic movement. To stay in required repentance and a transformation of the values that guided behavior. For Paul, they were called to a holiness grounded in the love of God and neighbor and empowered by the indwelling of God's Spirit. In his life and work, Paul's eschatological hopes became incarnated in Jesus communities that embodied Jesus' preaching and were a sign of rebuke to the Roman order and "the present evil age."

QUESTIONS FOR
REFLECTION AND DISCUSSION

1. What are people missing about Jesus' and Paul's preaching when they describe it simply as a personal or private spirituality?
2. In Paul's worldview, how did the event of resurrection and Gentiles fit together?
3. How was the *ekklēsia* an eschatological symbol?

Theological Perspective

Over the centuries every word, every idea in Paul's letters has been scrutinized and debated. Questions seek the meaning of his religious concepts and the realities to which they point. What did resurrection signify for him? What did Christ's death have to do with Gentiles? How did he conceive not only of sin, as acts or attitudes, but Sin, a power that binds? What did he mean by faith—faith in Christ or the faith of Christ? The interest in Paul has been intense throughout the tradition. The questions show no sign of drying up today.[1]

Today, more than ever before, scholars recognize that Paul was not a systematic thinker, but a man of deep conviction, passionately involved in ecclesiastical controversies with theological roots. In this chapter we hope to glimpse Paul's central convictions and his theological perspective by focusing on a cluster of terms having to do with Gentile believers and the redemptive import of the *ekklēsia*.[2]

PAUL'S GOSPEL

As we have seen, the term *gospel*, or *evangelion*, was a term used by the emperor for his announcements, the "good news" of a military victory or the birth of a royal child.

Paul proclaimed a gospel, too. He called it variously the "gospel of God" (Rom 1:1), "the gospel concerning his Son" (Rom 1:3), and the "gospel of Christ" (1 Thess 3:2). This gospel, unlike the imperial one that celebrated power and violence, announced that through Jesus came good news for the poor and marginalized: *God is for you.* His preaching and life illuminated the values that foster human well-being. This meaning of *gospel* is found more in the Synoptic Gospels than in Paul's letters.

Robert Jewett describes the good news in Paul as God's impartial righteousness. God's justice is that God treats all the same. Further, access to salvation is open. In his longest letter, to the Romans, Paul expressed his desire to proclaim the gospel to them. He summarized its content in this way:

> For I am not ashamed of the gospel; it is the power of God for salvation to everyone who has faith, to the Jew first and also to the Greek. (Rom 1:16–17)

Paul talks of righteousness in both divine and human terms. God's righteousness has to do with God's justice, as Jewett suggests above. "God shows no partiality" (Rom 2:11). God has provided the means of atonement for sins in Christ's death. The righteousness of God has been disclosed through faith in Christ for all who believe (3:22–23). Whether Paul is talking about "faith in Christ" or "faith of

Christ" is a debate among scholars. The latter leads to talking about Christ's obedience and his rectification of Adam's sin. Because of his sacrificial death, the means of atonement—forgiveness of sin—is provided. Righteousness is also applied on the human side. The believer is righteous—made right with God—through faith in Christ.

Paul understood himself as having a prophetic call with one task: to extend God's offer of salvation to Gentile women and men. He was to bring them into the eschatological Israel to the worship of the true God of Israel. Their inclusion would fulfill the biblical promise to Abraham that all nations would be included in Israel's covenant with God (Gen 17:4).

As sinners outside the covenant, the Gentiles' ability to accept God's offer was dependent on Christ's death. Jesus followers had already interpreted Jesus' death as a sacrifice prior to Paul's entry into the movement. The ritual of sacrifice, familiar to Jews from the Jerusalem Temple, was linked with atonement. It was through a sacrifice offered to God that the debt for sin was set aside and the right relation to God reestablished. Disciples of Jesus proclaimed that by his death, once and for all, Jesus paid back the debt humankind owed to God for sin.

Paul's preaching emphasized that the sacrificial death of Christ paid back the debt Gentiles owed for sin yet could never pay themselves. Freed by Jesus, Gentiles now stood in a position of being able to accept God's offer of salvation.

JUSTIFICATION

Paul's view broke decisively from the dominant view among Jews about Gentile inclusion in the eschatological time. The expectation was shared that Gentiles would someday come to worship the God of Israel. That was a biblical promise. But the prevailing Jewish opinion was that Gentiles would do this "the normal way," by becoming proselytes and, through full conversion, becoming Jewish women and men. Belonging was not separate from the law. E. P. Sanders has emphasized that the understanding in the first century was that it is acceptance of the covenant that establishes one in Israel and that accepting the covenant means obeying the commandments. In the Jesus movement itself, Larry Hurtado writes:

> Many, perhaps most, Jewish Christians seem generally to have found no incompatibility between putting faith in Jesus as Messiah and glorified Lord and continuing their traditional observance of Torah, which they still regarded as the commandments of God. Some Jewish Christians (the "circumcision party") demanded that Gentile believers, in addition to putting faith in Jesus also take up full observance of Torah. Otherwise they had not made a full conversion to the God of Israel.[3]

The importance given to Paul later in the tradition masks the fact that Paul's position on the inclusion of Gentiles was, at that time, the minority position and the Torah-observant position of James in Jerusalem the majority one. The tradition later reversed these positions, starting with the Gospel narratives themselves where the role of James virtually disappears.[4]

Paul did not insist on Gentile women and men doing the works of the law. They had been put in the right relation to God through Christ. This is one of the most familiar lines from Paul's letters: "For we hold that a person is justified by faith apart from works of the law" (Rom 3:28). Yet despite his very strong and hostile words about the law, Paul did not reject its validity as a way of life for Jews but rather the necessity of its adoption for Gentiles. Some argue that what Paul was opposing was the nationalistic use of the law to distinguish between Jew and Gentile.

Regardless of how the law functioned generally, what was salvific for both was faith in Christ. At the heart of Paul's theology of justification, E. P. Sanders writes, was the conviction "that Jesus Christ is Lord, that in him God has provided for the salvation of all who believe (in the general sense of 'be converted')."[5] Paul's affirmation in Romans expresses this conviction: "If you confess with your lips that Jesus is Lord and believe in your heart that God raised him from the dead, you shall be saved" (Rom 10:9). The equality of Jew and Gentile is grounded in their faith in Christ: "for in Christ Jesus you are all children of God through faith" (Gal 3:26). With Christ the law had been fulfilled: "For Christ is the end of the law so that there may be righteousness for everyone who believes" (Rom 10:4).

Alan Segal writes that Paul's conversion generated a new understanding of the covenant for Paul, yet he perceived himself as remaining within Judaism. Similarly, Calvin Roetzel emphasizes that Paul's "language, his Scriptures, his holy symbols, and his institutions were and remained Jewish."[6] But however grounded Paul was in Jewish faith, and however little he conceived of his ministry as forging ahead into a new religion, with this claim of the salvific significance of Christ Paul had in fact moved definitively out of an exclusivist theology of Jewish election into an equally exclusivist Christian one. Paul was perplexed as to why Jews did not respond to the proclamation of Christ. He asked in Romans if God has rejected his people. To this he said no. The hardened hearts that resisted Christ, however, had a function. They opened the way for Gentile faith. In time, when the "full number of the Gentiles has come," then the way will open "for all of Israel to be saved" (11:26). By the time he wrote Romans he had resolved the dilemma by seeing rejection and acceptance as necessary to God's plan that the faith of Gentiles would lead Israel to its profession of Christ.

Paul cautions believers not to confuse Jewish opposition to them with grounds for God's rejection of them. Their "gifts and the calling of God are irrevocable" (11:29). The election of Israel is permanent.

RELIGIOUS CONVERSION

By responding to Paul's preaching, Gentile women and men come into the eschatological assembly in the same way as he did, through religious conversion. Just as he shifted his loyalties from the Pharisees to the messianic Jews, so the loyalties of Gentiles shifted from the persons and religions of their past to the Christ-confessing assembly and to the God of Israel. The phrase *faith in Christ* denoted the experiential reality of conversion. Symbolically dying with Christ in the ritual of baptism freed believers from their enslavement to the power of sin. Belonging to Christ broke the bondage to a world of false meanings and values. The "old self was crucified" so that "sin might be destroyed" (Rom 6:5). The old self became the new self. For Gentiles, moral transformation was not contingent on fidelity to the law but on the indwelling of the Spirit: "God's love has been poured into our hearts through the Holy Spirit" (Rom 5:5).

The expectation of the Spirit runs deep in Jewish restoration eschatology. The giving of the Spirit would signify the restoration of creation. It would be a time when evil was overcome, including the evil of Israel's domination by foreign powers. But it was expected that the Spirit would be given to Jews and only in the context of law observance.

God's gift of the Spirit to Gentile women and men confirmed for Paul his position that God's acceptance of them was due to their faith in Christ. The blessing that had come to Abraham was now being extended to the Gentiles through their reception of the Spirit (Gal 3:14). Those who belong to Christ can live by and be guided by the Spirit. Its presence is known by its fruits, namely, "love, joy, peace, patience, kindness, generosity, faithfulness, gentleness, and self-control" (Gal 5:22). The way of life mandated by the Torah is not demanded of Gentiles, but the Spirit enables them to fulfill what had long been seen to be the deepest meaning of the law: love of God and love of neighbor (Lev 19:18; Mark 12:31). Paul now calls this the law of Christ: "Bear one another's burdens," he writes, "and in this way you will fulfill the law of Christ" (Gal 6:2).

EKKLĒSIA

Inclusion was a central value for Jesus. The Pauline assemblies appropriated this value by creating a new social reality that exchanged relations of domination for those of mutuality. *Ekklēsia*, the Greek term they appropriated for their assemblies, referred to the democratic assembly of free—meaning elite male—citizens in the Greek city.[7] The Jesus followers extended the meaning of citizens beyond elite males to profess the equality of all members of the assembly. This was a rejection of hierarchy, of the patriarchal family, and of rule. It was also a rejection of the artificial division of social reality into spheres of the privileged and the marginalized. Redemption was experienced as equality in participation and membership, equality as a person with others. Equality was intrinsic—not accidental—to redemption.

Paul designated these eschatological assemblies the "new covenant" (1 Cor 11:25; 2 Cor 3:6). In this covenant initiated by the death and resurrection of Christ, Paul contrasted Christ with Adam. Adam's disobedience set in motion the downward spiral of sin. Christ's obedience reversed this downward spiral and set in motion the restoration of creation. Belonging to Christ through baptism and the power of the Spirit freed the believer from the power of sin (Rom 7: 4–6). Paul conceived of these religious assemblies as an alternative social order. In Christ, in the *ekklēsia*, all are persons, none are nonpersons, none are to be exploited or possessed. The old order is dominated by sin; but the new one, as Paul tells the Corinthians, is: "When anyone is united to Christ, there is a new world; the old order is gone, and a new order has already begun" (2 Cor 5:17). The *ekklēsia* is a "new creation" (Gal 6:15). Elisabeth Schüssler Fiorenza writes:

> This inclusive character of the Jesus movement made it possible later to invite Gentiles of all nations into the Christian community, which transcended Jewish as well as Hellenistic

cultural and religious boundaries. In this new community, status distinctions were abolished, and neither fixed structures nor institutionalized leadership was present. These Christians understood themselves as the eschatological community and the representatives of the "new creation." They all had received the Holy Spirit and all were empowered by the Spirit to proclaim the great deeds of God in Jesus Christ.[8]

GROUP IDENTITY

For Second Temple Judaism, the Torah created a boundary between covenant insider and outsider, and for good reasons. James D. G. Dunn highlights the social function of the law in the context of Roman occupation and Hellenistic culture. Important boundary markers were the sign of the covenant, circumcision, Sabbath rest, and dietary practices. Dunn emphasizes that inclusion in the covenant required these observances, particularly those that marked the distinctiveness of the people of Israel from others.[9]

For Paul the Jesus follower and apocalyptic Jew, Alan Segal writes, baptism was the eschatological marker between insiders and outsiders. Access to God was no longer mediated by priests and through sacrifice in the Temple. Paul's images are immediate and personal: "being in Christ" (Rom 3:28; 5:5), "belonging to Christ" (Rom 7:4–6). The assembly is the "body of Christ" (Gal 3:25–29). Baptism functions as the Torah did to mark insiders and outsiders. Insiders are a "new creation" (Gal 6:15).

While there is some indication that men—or even women—brought their whole household with them when they became believers, it is thought that the more usual was the inclusion of individuals whose conversion brought them into the Christ-professing assembly. They entered into a charismatic community where roles and leadership reflected the "Spirit that is from God" (1 Cor 2:12) rather than the prerogatives of class or gender. They received spiritual gifts of wisdom and prophecy. "The Pauline concept of church and ministry," James Dunn writes, "*differs from the pattern that evolved at Jerusalem* in that it was essentially a concept of charismatic authority."[10] Pheme Perkins writes that women's Spirit-filled prophecy and possession of wisdom meant an enhanced social status.[11]

HOLINESS

Paul required the same thing of Gentile women and men that the biblical writers emphasized for Israel: holiness. Israel was to be holy as God is holy. Gentile believers were to be holy, too. Holiness includes morality, but it goes beyond it in the love of God and love of neighbor that transforms moral living. In the letter thought to be his earliest, Paul appeals to God to strengthen the hearts of the Thessalonian believers in holiness. They are to love one another (1 Thess 3:13, 4:10), just as in Leviticus, the people had been commanded to "love your neighbor as yourself" (Lev 19:18).

This conviction runs deep in Jewish tradition. The Deuteronomist linked loving God and following God's law with living: "love the LORD your God with all your heart and with all your soul, in order that you may live" (Deut 30:6). "If you obey the commandments of the LORD your God . . . then you shall live." The Psalmist praises God as the Creator, as the God of all nations, as the God who brought Israel out of slavery. Human destiny is wrapped up in the duty to praise this God and obey God's statutes: "Happy are those whose way is blameless, who walk in the law of the LORD. Happy are they who keep his decrees, who seek him with their whole heart, who also do no wrong, but walk in his ways" (Ps 119:1–3). Fidelity to the covenant requires living God's law. The psalms, too, link obeying God's commands with life: "I will never forget your precepts, for by them you have given me life" (Ps 119:93).

For Gentiles, developing holiness meant apprehending themselves differently than they were used to doing. After confronting problems of sexual behavior in the Corinthian assembly, Paul used the image of the Temple to emphasize the sacredness of the human person. The person is to be as holy as the Temple is holy (1 Cor 3:16–17). The Temple is holy because it is God's dwelling place. Paul tells the Corinthians that the body of each is a temple with the Holy Spirit dwelling within. They are to "glorify God in [their] body" (6:15–20). Paul lists various sins that violate that holiness.

The means of achieving holiness were different for Paul and the biblical writers. Both grounded righteousness first in the orientation of persons and communities to the God of Israel. For Israel this orientation then demanded observance of God's law as given to Moses. But Paul instructs Gentiles to "live by the Spirit" (Gal 5:16). The power of the Spirit offsets the power of sin (5:16–21), opening the heart to seek and do what is good. The indwelling of divine reality generates and sustains moral transformation. The authenticity engendered by the Spirit counters the unauthenticity generated by sin. As we have seen, the fruits of the Spirit are "love, joy, peace, patience, kindness, generosity, faithfulness, gentleness, and self-control" (5:22).

ONE IN CHRIST

The diversity of their gifts of the Spirit is unified by the Spirit into "one body" (1 Cor. 12:12–13). The community is the body of Christ and each a member of it (12:12, 27).

Paul's images for the inclusiveness and equality of the *ekklēsia* are striking: "being in Christ," "body of Christ," "new covenant," "new creation." He extended the boundaries of Israel's covenant community to include all believers, when before the covenant had included only the people of Israel as the elect. While he did not see himself as abandoning Judaism with this position, he effectively went beyond the limit of what inclusion could bear and have the group self-definition still hold. To be in Israel's covenant and not observe the law was a contradiction in terms for most.

Paul's impulses were inclusionary and, with a few exceptions, genuinely gender-neutral. In his passionate defense of his gospel to the Galatians, not a hint of difference between women and men believers arises, although he focuses rather directly on men in his remark that he hoped that "those upsetting you might also castrate themselves!" (Gal 5:12).

But however inclusionary Paul himself was with regard to the assembly, his message is effectively an exclusionary one. There is one way to God: Jesus Christ. Acts 4:12 is a classic statement of the early Christian understanding of salvation:

> And there is salvation in no one else, for there is no other name under heaven given among men by which we must be saved. (Acts 4:12)

While the language of election can be very moving, there is a dark side to it as well. As we see in the discussion of the Christian *adversus Judaeos* tradition in chapter 7, the category of election grants only one group truth and value.

QUESTIONS FOR
REFLECTION AND DISCUSSION

1. How did Paul's gospel reflect his consuming interest? How was his belief different even from some other Jesus followers? Why would Jews have opposed it?
2. Is it correct to say that Paul rejected the law? What do we need to add?
3. How did Paul expect Gentiles to come into the eschatological community? How were they to live? What substituted for the Torah in ethical guidance?

The Truth of the Gospel

Paul's reputation as the outstanding and enthusiastic evangelist of the early Jesus movement and the respected status of his New Testament letters mask the historical reality that Paul's importance actually came later in the Christian tradition and was projected back into his own time. Calvin Roetzel calls Paul a "marginal Jew," which seems an odd designation given Paul's present status but not if we are thinking historically.[1]

The same may be said of Paul's reputation as a Pharisee. No doubt Paul identified with Pharisaism and, by virtue of a profound personal experience, he shifted his loyalties from a Pharisaic to a messianic form of Judaism. But the exalted status implied by associating him with the respected Rabbi Gamaliel (Acts 22:3)[2] reflects more the desire of the writer of Acts to align Paul with an important figure—one whose intervention saved the apostles' lives (Acts 5:13–42)—rather than historical biography.[3] Paul was likely a "marginal Pharisee" and not one who studied with the famous or did the business of the high priest and the Sanhedrin (Acts 9:1–3).

Of all Paul's letters, Galatians is a front-runner in the "most interpreted" category. It is famous for Paul's valiant defense of salvation for Gentiles and for his contrast between works of the law and faith in Christ. The *adversus Judaeos* tradition later will interpret Paul's addition of the Gentiles as exclusion of the Jews and interpret his contrast of works and faith as a comparison between two kinds of religions instead of two conditions for Gentile inclusion in the covenant community of Israel. But Paul was not thinking about two religions. His hands were full just trying to defend what he believed divinely revealed, that is, that the death of Christ had taken away the Gentiles' debt for sin and they were reconciled to God, not as Jews but as they were.

We take up in this chapter one of the many crises Paul faced during his ministry. But it is not the crisis itself that distinguishes Galatians from his other letters. One could safely say that crisis occasioned each letter. Rather, it is that this particular crisis—a deliberate undermining of Paul's preaching—had reached such proportions that Paul was fearful that his opponents were very close to winning his converts in Galatia over to "a different gospel." This opposition to Paul did not come from outside the messianic community but from within. The letter shows us the wide range in messianic views in the beginning stages of the Jesus movement. The conflict was not over two kinds of religion but ultimately two types of assemblies.

PROBLEMS, QUESTIONS, CONFLICTS

Separated from communities he had founded by missionary journeys and periodic imprisonment, Paul had few options for advising or encouraging these assemblies other than letter writing. Rhetoric was a substitute for physical presence. Paul's letters capture the pressures these assemblies were under. External pressures could threaten a community's very survival. But it was often the internal pressures created by the behavior of members themselves that endangered the harmony of an assembly. Paul put all of his powers of persuasion to work in resolving whatever difficulties were reported to him.

Lacking the original letters or messages sent to Paul from the assemblies, we have to reconstruct the historical situations from his responses. It is easy to misunderstand the meanings and values of persons in cultures other than our own. If the original situation is misunderstood, Paul's response will be misunderstood as well.

Paul wrote far more than generic letters of advice or encouragement. He sought in each to meet the exigence of a new question or problem with a response that was at once personal, ethical, and theological. His theological worldview developed in relation to these new questions. When members of their assembly started dying, for example, the Thessalonians became anxious because Paul had led them to believe that Christ would return in judgment during their lives and that they would be raised to new life then (1 Thess 4:13–5:11). In response, Paul expanded his original idea of the day of the Lord, assuring the Thessalonians that Christ would raise those who had died first and then those who were still alive. This new dimension of his theology of resurrection was worked out because a new question demanded a new answer. In Galatians, Paul was pressed to defend "the truth of the gospel" as he presented it to Galatian women and men in a bitter controversy over conditions of Gentile membership.

The Galatian crisis was created by the arrival of what in better circumstances would be called Paul's fellow evangelists. Given the bitter way he talks about them, it is clear that they are not friends. These evangelists have come into assemblies that Paul founded to challenge the truth of his gospel. By presenting what he called a "different gospel," they introduced doubt about the credibility of Paul's gospel.

Paul poured himself into the creation of a persuasive argument against this different gospel. His letter is as often eloquent and touching as it is unfair and mean-spirited. His negative characterization of these evangelists was taken in the tradition as historical description. E. P. Sanders writes that this polemical caricature of these evangelists made it difficult for subsequent Christians to see that theirs was "an entirely reasonable position."[4]

Paul had good reason to fear these evangelists. Their case was strong; they had scripture and authority on their side. The depth of Paul's anxiety shows in his outbursts, such as wishing those who were preaching the necessity of circumcision for Gentile converts would castrate themselves (5:12) and the double curse he put on them (1:8–9). If enough of the Galatian believers were convinced by this argument of the other evangelists, the assembly would be changed dramatically. Paul was right in saying that if the

Gentile men allowed themselves to be circumcised, they were obliged to obey the entire law (5:3). This obligation is the privilege of the covenant insider, both as Jewish and as male. Accepting the circumcision preaching would create a Torah-observant assembly, for women as well as men. As Paul knew the scriptures would show, God gave Israel the law as the means of fidelity to the covenant God had established with Israel.[5] There was a radical difference between the assembly Paul had founded and the one the Galatians were being asked to adopt. He voiced his fear that they were "forsaking" him (1:6), but also that they would be forsaking the vision of community he had shaped for them as well.

THE RECIPIENTS

In one way it is simple to say who received this letter: women and men whom Paul had converted with his proclamation of Christ. They are thought to be all Gentiles. In fact, as E. P. Sanders argues, there is no evidence of Jews in any of the Pauline communities. The assembly in Rome was mixed, but it was not founded by Paul.

The number of women and men drawn to Paul's preaching must have been sizable enough or spread over an area large enough to warrant establishing several assemblies. Paul addresses the letter to "the churches in Galatia" (1:2). We do not know where the Galatian assemblies were. Galatia was a Roman province, a region, not a city. Exactly how the Romans drew the boundaries of the province is unclear.[6] Hans Dieter Betz describes the Galatians as inhabitants of the central plateau of Asia Minor. The rhetorical and theological sophistication of the letter suggests to him that the recipients were Hellenized and Romanized, as well as urban and educated.

While the women and men Paul converted were Gentiles, they may have already been associated with the synagogue when they heard Paul preach. Some Gentiles were known as God fearers, that is, persons who adopted Jewish beliefs, values, and practices but who had stopped just short of full conversion.[7] What attracted Gentiles? Louis Feldman offers one possibility:

> Many undoubtedly were attracted, in a period of general political, economic, and social instability to a community which, by regulating itself, had found inner security. The fellowship which came through eating together, attending weekly meetings, and avoiding the same foods may have enticed the lonely.[8]

Among Gentiles, Jews were admired for the antiquity of their beliefs, for their loyalty to their one God, Yahweh, and for their moral lifestyle. They welcomed Gentiles at Diaspora synagogues. "But they could be treated as full members of the Jewish people," Larry Hurtado writes, "only if they made a proper conversion that involved a commitment to observance of Torah (e.g., Sabbath, food laws, and for males, circumcision)."[9] Paul's use of Scripture in the letter assumes that the recipients are familiar with the stories. It assumes, too, that a figure like Abraham would command respect. Paul's Galatian converts may have been God fearers.

E. P. Sanders describes the law-based spirituality of Second Temple Judaism as "covenantal nomism." For both native-born Israelites and Gentile proselytes, "*accepting* the covenant both requires and is evidenced by *obeying* the commandments. It is the acceptance of the covenant which establishes one in Israel." The proper proselyte, Sanders writes, "is a *ger tsaddiq*, a 'righteous proselyte' because like a righteous native-born Israelite he obeys the Torah."[10] He sums up the meaning of Torah observance in this way:

> For the principle on which the law rests is perfectly clear: God gave the Torah to Israel by the hand of Moses; obedience to the Torah is the condition for retaining covenant promises; intentional and unrepenting disobedience implies rejection of the law, rejection of the covenant for which it is the condition, and rejection of the God who gave the law and the covenant.[11]

THE EKKLĒSIA

The women and men who responded to Paul formed an *ekklēsia*, a discipleship community of equals, as Elisabeth Schüssler Fiorenza calls them.[12] In social science terminology they were a "fictive kinship group," related to one another through a shared conversion experience and religious horizon. The *ekklēsia* shares features of the Diaspora synagogue.

Women and men entered into the assembly through the same initiation ritual of baptism. Religious experience of divine reality was primary. The term *charisma* is associated with the gift of the Holy Spirit,[13] and the Jesus movement was a charismatic movement. Members received God's gift of the Spirit through baptism. They were governed by those with charismatic authority. Functions and roles within the community were differentiated as gifts of the Spirit. The power underlying their moral transformation was the indwelling of the Holy Spirit. The assembly was characterized by charismatic equality. There was an absence of gender difference in the participation and leadership of women and men.

For Paul, that God had given God's Spirit to the Gentiles confirmed that God now accepted Gentiles as Gentiles. No longer were they required to become Jewish in order to share in the covenant of Israel. The condition of their coming into the covenant was faith in Christ.

Women entered into the discipleship community as individuals and generally not as a part of a father's or husband's household. Many of the women Paul named in his letters are named alone and not in relation to a man; presumably they are unmarried (cf. Rom 16). Some women are named individually as benefactors to Paul such as Phoebe, who is a deacon of the assembly in Cenchreae and delivers Paul's letter to the Romans (Rom 1:1).

Women acted independently in joining these Pauline communities. They had prominent roles in the early Jesus movement. In this they were like women in Greco-Roman religions and Jewish women in Diaspora synagogues.[14] Karen Jo Torjesen shows the way in which women's roles in public worship in Greek society were well established.[15] They served as priestesses in different religions. In Roman society, the most important of the official cults was the College of Vestal Virgins. Women were an accepted part of religious leadership in both societies. Bernadette Brooten cites archaeological evidence—inscriptions naming women as *presbyters* (elders)—of the involvement of Jewish women in Diaspora synagogues.[16] The leadership of women in the Pauline communities appears to have been in continuity with women's roles in Jewish public life.

We have to hold two disparate facts about women in mind at the same time. One fact is that social norms, legal codes, and religious texts define women as the property of men, restrict them to private and domestic space, and subordinate them to the rule of men as inferior to superior beings. The Torah defines women as the property of men— a standard feature of the ancient patriarchal world—and its commands created separate and unequal gender spheres. The second fact is the evident independence and participation of women in Greco-Roman and Jewish religions.

To account for these two disparate facts in Judaism, Shaye Cohen draws the distinction between Judaism as legislated and Judaism as practiced. Second Temple Judaism as practiced, he writes, did not correspond exactly to Judaism as prescribed in biblical and postbiblical texts.[17] The texts prescribe subordination and seclusion, yet the reality is that women often were independent and in public. It is a both/ and rather than an either/or. Ross Kraemer writes:

> Rabbinic writings have led many scholars to conclude that Jewish women led restricted, secluded lives and were excluded from much of the rich ritual life of Jewish men, especially from the study of Torah. Evidence from the Greco-Roman Diaspora suggests, however, that at least some Jewish women played active religious, social, economic, and even political roles in the public lives of Jewish communities.[18]

The Pauline assemblies were emancipatory groups in which the meaning of redemption was linked to equality. Women and men participated in the same way. Paul cites what scholars believe to be a fragment from the assembly's baptismal ceremony:

> There is no longer Jew or Greek, there is no longer slave or free, there is no longer male and female; for all of you are all one in Christ Jesus. (Gal 3:28)

This is a packed sentence. We could decode it in the following way:

- "In Christ Jesus" = "in the assembly"
- In the assembly = no longer privileged
- "One" = equal
- "One in Christ Jesus" = equal in the assembly
- "no longer" = sin = privilege
- without privilege = redemptive equality

OTHER EVANGELISTS

Who were these people whom Paul calls by such names as "false brothers," "false preachers," the "superapostles," or "those with a different gospel"? What is signaled by identifying them as "men from James"?

For much of the tradition it was assumed that these visitors were Jews, in contrast to Paul, who had become Christian. They were outsiders to Christianity; he was an influential insider. Called legalists and hypocrites, the visitors were accused of "work-righteousness," that is, of thinking that they could merit their own salvation—force God's hand, so to speak—by following all the rules even if the spirit of truth and goodness, not to say the love of God, was missing from their spirituality. They were described as "Judaizers," a description that conveys a slur, as if "Judaizing" was forcing some sort of improper behavior on someone. They preached the law while Paul preached freedom.

This traditional story of the difference between Paul and these men has been rejected by all but the most fundamentalist Christians and those who, in the past half century, have not taken the time to understand the nature of Christian supersessionism or Christian theological anti-Semitism. We have the outlines of the ideological bias in this short narrative, and it will be the subject of chapter 7.

But the visitors were insiders, not outsiders. They were evangelists like Paul. The Galatian conflict is first and foremost an insider conflict. They represented different wings of the Jesus movement. Paul's wing is in the Diaspora. The others are from the Palestinian wing. "Men from James" would be from the Jerusalem assembly where James was.

Paul's use of adjectives such as *false* or the sarcasm that accompanies terms such as *superapostles* is simply polemical. It is intended to do what polemics always do—distort situations, ridicule one's opponents, sway one's audience toward a certain viewpoint. Paul uses these terms as part of a strategy to convince the Galatian believers that his presentation of the Gospel is right and that of the other evangelists wrong. Polemical rhetoric is never concerned about being fair.

It would be inaccurate, though, if we were under the impression that these evangelists disagreed with Paul about everything. They have more in common with him than we usually credit. We will review their agreements first and then turn toward their point of conflict.

AGREEMENTS, DISAGREEMENTS

The evangelists on both sides of the Galatian conflict shared the main features of Jewish eschatological theology. On these points they were of the same mind. Agreements:

- God raised the crucified Jesus from the dead, validated his person and message, anointed him Messiah, and signaled the beginning of the end time, the *eschaton*.
- In the end time God would counter the dominance of evil; already the imperial power that had crucified Jesus had been rendered void.
- Divine judgment was right around the corner; Jesus would return to punish evildoers—empires as well as individuals—and vindicate the righteous.
- Now is the time for repentance and holiness.
- All nations will worship the true God, fulfilling the biblical promise to Abraham.

Disagreements: The Palestinian and Diaspora evangelists went separate ways on the question of the inclusion of Gentiles.

- How do Gentiles come into the covenant community of Israel?

- What do they have to do to stay in?
- Must Gentiles become Jewish in order to follow Jesus and join the *ekklēsia*?

They are "from James," meaning from James, the brother of Jesus, in Jerusalem. James was called "the Just" because of his fidelity to the law.[19] James's answer to the question of Gentile inclusion is indicated by his personal commitment to Torah observance. It is the condition for justification. As a leader in the Jerusalem assembly, James's understanding of the eschatological assembly would have carried much authority. In terms of Gentiles, this meant that things are the same for them: if they want to share in the biblical promises to Israel, they must observe Torah to become Jewish and be included in Israel's covenant.

By explicitly calling for circumcision (5:2, 6:12), the Jerusalem evangelists have challenged Paul at the basis of his understanding of Gentile inclusion, in particular, his belief that living the way of the law was not necessary for Gentiles. The visitors surely cited James's position—one they shared—that the obligation God had given to live the way of the law had not changed with the advent of Jesus. The first command of the covenant regarded the sign of the covenant:

> This is my covenant, which you shall keep, between me and you and your offspring after you: Every male among you shall be circumcised. . . . [This] shall be a sign of the covenant between me and you. . . . Any uncircumcised male who is not circumcised in the flesh of his foreskin shall be cut off from his people; he has broken my covenant. (Gen 17:11–14)

If Gentile males wanted to come into Israel, they were welcome. But first they had to fulfill the conditions for being a member. Faithfulness to God required fidelity to this and other commands. This position was easily backed by Scripture. The visitors could point the Galatian believers to Deuteronomy and elsewhere in the Torah to confirm that the law was necessary:

> So now, O Israel, what does the Lord your God require of you? Only to fear the Lord your God, to walk in all his ways, to love him, to serve the Lord your God with all your heart and with all your soul, and to keep the commandments of the Lord your God and his decrees that I am commanding you today, for your own well-being. (Deut 10:12–13)

> See, I am setting before you today a blessing and a curse: the blessing, if you obey the commandments of the Lord your God that I am commanding you today; and the curse, if you do not obey the commandments of the Lord your God, but turn from the way that I am commanding you today. (Deut 11:26–28)

> This very day the Lord your God is commanding you to observe these statutes and ordinances; so observe them diligently with all your heart and with all your soul. Today you have obtained the Lord's agreement: to be your God; and for you to walk in his ways, to keep his statutes, his commandments, and his ordinances, and to obey him. Today the Lord has obtained your agreement: to be his treasured people, as he promised you, and to keep his commandments; for him to set you high above all nations that he has made, in praise and in honor; and for you to be a people holy to the Lord your God as he promised. (Deut 26:16–19)

The texts are clear. Fidelity to the covenant requires living the way of the Torah. Paul's preaching of freedom from the law begins to look suspect.

Paul's dispute with the other evangelists was ostensibly over whether Gentile males must be circumcised to participate in the *ekklēsia*. Circumcision refers to a physical act, but it is also a cipher for doing the works of the law.[20] The call of the evangelists for circumcision was relevant for women as well as men; do the works of the law. But the commands were different for each. Men were obligated— they had the privilege—to observe the whole law, as Paul says (5:3). Women were exempt from this obligation— they were denied the privilege—of keeping the whole law but observed those commands specifically addressed to women.[21]

Palestinian Judaism was shaped by influence of the Pharisees, the centrality of the rabbi, and the expectation of full conversion for Gentiles attracted to Judaism. The rabbinic expectation was that Gentiles would become full proselytes and, upon becoming Jewish, would be fully Torah observant. The Pharisees and rabbis interpreted the Torah more conservatively—for example, regarding women—than did Diaspora Jews.

In Diaspora Judaism, however, synagogues were led by laypersons rather than rabbis. Men and women shared public roles and offices. They held a broader range of views regarding Gentile inclusion.

Palestinian and Diaspora messianism mirrored these differences between Palestinian and Diaspora Judaism. The Palestinian evangelists presumed a strict adherence to

Torah. Their call for circumcision reinforced gender difference in membership and practice. The Diaspora assemblies, on the other hand, were led by laypersons; women and men shared roles and offices, and a more liberal interpretation was given to Torah mandates. The Palestinian evangelists' call for circumcision reasserted gender difference in the Diaspora assemblies.

FAITH IN CHRIST

Paul's position on Gentile inclusion was an extreme one. In the first century, as Dunn remarks, the law was coterminous with Judaism.[22] It would have been impossible for most to conceive of Judaism without the law or to think of membership in the covenant people apart from the law. Paul's rejection of circumcision for Gentile men and his rejection of living the way of the law for both Gentile women and men—and yet he considered them "in"—would have threatened the self-identity of people as Jews.

The Jesus followers in Antioch whom Paul joined after his mystical experience of Christ shared table fellowship with Gentiles in their house meetings (2:11). In his letter to the Galatians, Paul begins his rebuttal to the Jerusalem evangelists by telling a story of another (or the same) group of "men from James" coming to Antioch (2:11–14).[23] Peter, who was then in Antioch, had been sharing a ritual meal with Gentiles. But when the Torah-observant Jesus followers came, Peter withdrew from associating with the Gentile members of the assembly out of fear of the judgment of these men. In an angry public confrontation Paul called Peter a hypocrite.

Paul makes a point of saying at the beginning of his letter that he had cleared his position on Gentile inclusion with the apostles in Jerusalem—first with Peter and James and then fourteen years later with unnamed leaders (1:18–19). He had presented his case, and they had shaken hands in agreement with him. As evidence of their sincerity Paul notes that the Jerusalem leaders had not compelled Paul's missionary companion, Titus, "though he was Greek," to be circumcised (2:3). They had agreed with Paul on the "truth of the gospel" (2:5, 2:14–16). But the appearance of opponents to Paul's preaching in the Galatian assemblies and elsewhere demonstrates that some at least were ready to reevangelize his assemblies and turn them around, into communities that met the requirements for covenant fidelity.

By grounding his authority in Jesus Christ and God the Father (1:1, 12), Paul implicitly offsets the authority of James. Instead of seeing fidelity to God in either Jewish or Gentile terms ("circumcision or uncircumcision"), Paul raises the image of the eschatological assembly as a "new creation": "For neither circumcision or uncircumcision is anything; but a new creation is everything!" (6:15).

Paul rejected the claim that Gentile men must be circumcised to be full members of the covenant community. But he did not argue that Jewish men no longer were required to do so. He was not saying that Jewish women and men should not live the way of the law. What Paul said about the law was relevant to the inclusion of Gentile women and men. Paul was convinced that God was offering Gentiles salvation through Jesus and that becoming Jewish through conversion was no longer necessary. This was the "truth of the gospel" (3:14).[24]

Whether Paul saw the call for circumcision as nationalism or a form of ethnic exclusivity is open to debate. But from his mystical experience of the risen Christ he was convinced that Christ mediated the reconciliation of Gentiles to God, and their reorientation to the God of Israel was sufficient as a means of justification. Paul referred to the dynamics of conversion by the shorthand phrase "faith in Christ" (2:16–17). Hearing the Christ proclamation promoted religious conversion, and in turn conversion brought Gentiles to baptism and initiation into the assembly as members. This is how Gentiles "come into" Israel. They stay in by their lives of holiness. God's gift of God's Spirit at baptism verified for Paul that his position was correct (3:2). Gentile adoption of Jewish practices would be a countersign to faith in the risen Christ (5:2–4).

The key components of Paul's argument are as follows. Coming into the covenant:

- "Just as Abraham 'believed God, and it was reckoned to him as righteousness,' so those who believe are the descendants of Abraham" (Gal 3:6).
- "Those who believe are blessed with Abraham who believed" (3:9).
- "We ourselves are Jews by birth and not Gentile sinners yet we know that a person is justified not by the works of the law but through faith in Jesus Christ" (2:15).

Living in the covenant:

- "Live by the Spirit" (5:16). "The fruit of the Spirit is love, joy, peace, patience, kindness, generosity, faithfulness, gentleness, and self-control" (5:22–23).

- "Let us work for the good of all, and especially for those of the family of faith" (6:10).
- "Bear one another's burdens, and in this way you will fulfill the law of Christ" (6:2).

For much of the Christian tradition, Galatians has been interpreted through a supersessionist lens. The other evangelists were bad; Paul was good. The law was bad; faith was good. Doing the works of the law was bad; living by faith in Christ was good. Circumcision was seen as a crude physical sign of the covenant. Missed in this interpretation was the fact that the conflict was over membership. That the Galatian assemblies included women and that the Jerusalem evangelists were insisting on a masculine-specific sign of membership was ignored. In fact, women became invisible. Interpreters routinely connect the terms Galatians and Gentiles with a phrase such as "those who would be circumcised." But the data to be taken into account are these:

- Galatians and Gentiles are both men and women.
- Faith in Christ and works of the law are mutually exclusive conditions for membership.
- Circumcision is a masculine-specific sign of full membership in the covenant community.[25]

If, in Paul's communities, membership in Israel was no longer linked to the gender-differentiated obligations of Torah, Elisabeth Schüssler Fiorenza writes, "women became full members of the people of God with the same rights and duties." This generated a fundamental change "not only in their standing before God but also in their ecclesial-social status and function, because in Judaism religious differences according to the law were also expressed in communal behavior and social practice." The Jesus movement was "based not on racial and national inheritance and kinship lines, but on a new kinship with Jesus Christ."[26]

CONSEQUENCES

Why did the Jerusalem evangelists come into the Diaspora assemblies? Under the umbrella of their call for circumcision, we can infer that they came to oppose the acceptance of Gentiles without full conversion into Israel and to make Gentile believers Gentile proselytes. We can presume they came to oppose the acceptance of uncircumcised Gentile males as members of Israel. Can we presume that the call for circumcision was also a reassertion of male privilege? Did they come specifically to reverse the equality affirmed in these communities? Did they come to oppose the acceptance of Gentile women as full members of Israel? Were they scandalized by table fellowship that placed not only Jewish and Gentile men in relations of equality but Jewish and Gentile men in a relation of equality with Gentile women? What difference would it have made to the Galatian assemblies if the members had accepted the Jerusalem evangelists' gospel? One consequence would have been the reinstatement of privilege.

First, acceptance of circumcision would have reconstructed the "fence" around Israel: Jews are insiders to the covenant; Gentiles are outsiders. Salvation is belonging. If

Gentile men and women want to share in Israel's salvation, they have to become Jewish men and women. Religious privilege would be reinstated.

Second, acceptance of circumcision would reconstruct the fence inside Israel. Circumcision separates men from women. It designates men—native-born and Jewish proselytes—as full members and gives them the obligation to follow the whole law. Gender privilege would be reinstated.

Jewish feminist scholars note that the Torah and the Mishnah, a postbiblical work of interpretation of the Torah, are patriarchal documents. The command to observe the whole law was given to the free adult male Israelite by birth and the male Gentile proselyte by conversion, a privilege denied to women.[27] The right to observe the law or the lack thereof given by the Torah itself created "separate and unequal spheres for women and men."[28]

In an analysis of the Mishnah, Judith Wegner argues that the Torah provided the precedents for the view of women and cultic obligations:

> Women simply do not count as full members of the community. Minors, slaves, and even foreigners (proselytes) can outgrow or otherwise overcome their respective handicaps and qualify as full Israelites; a woman never can.[29]

Wegner sums up the status of Jewish women: "Though Israelite-born, [women] rank, here, below proselytes and freedmen—non-Israelites by birth who later acquire that status."[30]

Ross Kraemer notes in relation to rabbinic texts that the "intensification of prescriptions against women is often a response to the increased autonomy and authority of women."[31] Her point may serve as an analogy to the Galatian situation. Did the Jerusalem evangelists come into the Galatian assemblies specifically to neutralize Paul's view that not only religious privilege but gender privilege had been abolished in the new Israel?

For Paul, the "truth of the gospel" was God's acceptance of Gentiles as Gentiles, that is, as Gentile men and Gentile women. Paul refused a masculine-specific condition of membership. He rejected gender difference. Everything he says about the status of Gentile believers, he says of both women and men.

In Paul's view, the eschatological gift of the Spirit creates a covenant community in which both females and males are full members (3:2, 26). Belonging is first contingent on religious conversion and the confirmation of conversion through baptism and the gift of the Spirit. Paul's whole vision of Christian community was at stake in the Galatian controversy.

QUESTIONS FOR
REFLECTION AND DISCUSSION

1. To what is Paul referring when he uses the phrase "truth of the gospel"? How did the Jerusalem Jesus followers think differently about this than Paul? Should we think of them as the "bad guys"?

2. What did circumcision signify? From where did Jews derive its authority as a symbol? Who would have

had the stronger argument on this issue—Paul or his fellow evangelists from Jerusalem? Why?

3. If the men had accepted circumcision, as the Jerusalem evangelists encouraged them to do, why would this have made any difference to women believers or to the *ekklēsia* itself?

Paul's Letters

P aul's letters offer us a glimpse into the inner dynamics of the Christ-professing assemblies he founded and his relationship with them. With some groups he is on congenial and warm terms, but with others his relationship is strained by painful memories barely hidden under the niceties of greetings and well wishes.

Limited by distance from these communities, Paul draws on his powers of persuasion to confront the difficulties they are undergoing. His response is both theological and ethical. His eschatological horizon places them in the "in-between time." The resurrection event has announced the beginning of God's intervention in history, and judgment remains yet ahead. This time between resurrection and judgment carries a moral imperative: to live rightly, to forgo false values and embrace genuine ones, and to let the indwelling of the Spirit transform one's moral horizon and behavior. Paul admonishes the Corinthian community, for example, for their "jealousy and quarreling" (1 Cor 3:3).

Because Paul's theological reflection was so rich, it was easy for subsequent readers to overlook the occasional nature of the letters and to read the letters as if they were theological treatises on grace or salvation unconnected with time or place or real persons. But to separate the content of his letters from the very particular contexts to which they were directed invites misunderstanding. Interpretation requires not only attending to what was said and how it was said but also recovering the historical setting in which these words took on certain meanings.

Words and ideas undergo changes throughout the history of their use. In the course of the Christian tradition, for example, resurrection became a proof of Jesus' divinity. When we read Paul's letters, however, we will want to recover how resurrection was a signal for Paul of the *eschaton*, the end time, and the ideas connected with the eschatological time, such as the inclusion of Gentiles. All nations will worship the true God, the God of Israel. Paul's experience of God giving him the mission to preach to the Gentiles makes more sense in this context. Resurrection and Gentiles are already connected. The more thoroughly we understand the historical setting, the more we can begin to see the world as Paul saw it. Did he see himself as part of a new religion? No. As participating in the end time? Yes.

CRUCIAL CAUTIONS

The intense scholarly scrutiny to which Paul's letters have been subjected over the past half century has uncovered interpretations in the tradition that rely on assumptions Paul did not have himself. Some discoveries have been difficult to appropriate because they challenge meanings that have become intertwined with Christian doctrinal truths themselves. If the underlying meaning of Paul's contrast between faith in Christ and works of the law, for example, is that a religion of grace (faith) is superior to a religion of law (works), then this assumption of superiority has no foundation when scholars demonstrate that faith in Christ and works of the law were two mutually exclusive conditions for Gentile membership in the covenant community of Israel. It is not easy simply to substitute meanings when the incorrect meaning has become a truth of faith itself, in this case the mistaken judgments that Christians have made about the exclusive validity of Christianity and the invalidity of Judaism.

Out of contemporary studies came a number of crucial insights, for example, into what is anachronistic and belongs to a later time and not to Paul himself. Many assumptions we have about Paul we bring to the text. What we think we see may not be there. They require critique and reevaluation. The insights may thus be stated as five cautions.

Seeing Christianity

In the course of recovering the Jewish context of Paul and the Jesus movement, contemporary scholars have contested the dominant assumption of the tradition that Paul perceived himself as an evangelist for a new religion. It became clearer that Christianity was not an immediate consequence of the death and resurrection of Christ but a development that took place over several decades, even a century or more. The separation of messianic Jews from other Jews was more pronounced after the catastrophe of the destruction of Jerusalem and the Temple at the end of the Jewish-Roman war in 70 C.E. Two Jewish parties competed for the allegiance of the Jewish people, Pharisaic Judaism and messianic Judaism. They became, in the second century, respectively, Rabbinic Judaism and Christianity.

While Paul added significantly to this development, he did not think of himself as contributing to the emergence of a new religion. As a religious entity distinct from Judaism, Christianity is a second-century phenomenon—at least forty years after the death of Paul. He is not Christian as opposed to Jewish. Paul's language of "being in Christ" reflects a kind of participation rather than a kind of institutional affiliation. He considered the Gentile assemblies he founded to be within the religious horizon of Israel (Gal 6:16). His own prophetic call occasioned a change of allegiance for himself, but this change was within Second Temple Judaism, not outside of it. Calvin Roetzel has emphasized that

> it is misleading to speak of Paul as a convert or apostate from Judaism. His language, his Scriptures, his holy symbols, and his institutions were and remained Jewish, and his personal reflections suggest a continuing attachment. Certainly there were tensions between Paul and his Jewish peers, but those were tensions that inevitably came from being a liminal or marginal figure. They were intra-mural, not extra-mural. In sum, Paul was born a Jew, lived as a Jew, and in all likelihood died as a Jew.[1]

Roetzel emphasizes that Paul "nowhere repudiated his native religion. And had he repudiated one expression of Judaism, would that mean he repudiated all Judaisms?"[2]

Seeing Hypocrites

Further insights uncovered the polemical rhetoric found in both Paul and the Gospels. Ultimately this hostile language reflects intra-Jewish tensions between Jewish Jesus followers and Jews who rejected their message. It intends to portray opponents and their views in the worst possible light. For much of the tradition these descriptions were thought to correspond with the "way things were."[3] In Paul's writings, opponents who came into his assemblies were subject to bitter and mean description, as in Philippians: "Beware of the dogs, beware of the evil workers, beware of those who mutilate the flesh!" (3:2). In the later Gospels, the Pharisees and scribes were depicted as self-righteous, hypocritical, and even evil. That they were well-meaning people seems almost impossible to believe.

Modern scholars question the assumption that a text mirrors history. Writers have interests, as ideological critics have emphasized. Writers engage in polemical description—not simply historical description—because they want persons or events to be understood in ways that are favorable to their own interests. Speaking of this negative view of the Pharisees and others, E. P. Sanders challenges the veracity of the traditional assumptions: "I have argued that this view is completely wrong: it proceeds from theological presuppositions and is supported by systematically misunderstanding and misconstruing passages in Rabbinic literature."[4] The androcentrism of texts that describe women negatively—or leave them out completely—is another standard way in which historical reality has been distorted by the interests of the writer. Negative description of others should generate suspicion that the author's interests have something to do with having the reader see persons or events in a particular way. To accept this description as an account of what the other was really like misunderstands not only the other but the writer as well. What is the writer doing? Why?

Seeing Legalism

For most of the tradition, commentators have read Paul and have "seen the legalism" that Paul hated so much. Until the influential work of E. P. Sanders published in 1977, *Paul and Palestinian Judaism*, Christian commentators assumed that Paul rejected the law. What was clarified by Sanders and others is that Paul did not reject the law as such—or even see Torah observance as legalism—but rather, he rejected the necessity of Gentile women and men becoming Jewish by their adoption of the law. He rejected a dominant idea of how Gentiles were to share in the salvation offered by God to Israel.

James D. G. Dunn put this in sociological rather than theological terms. The "social function of the law," Dunn argues, refers to "its national function as the civil and criminal code of the Jews as a distinct ethnic group." The phrase "works of the law" referred to the praxis the law laid upon the covenant member.[5] "Doing works of the law" simply meant "living as a Jew." Works of the law characterizes what Sanders calls "covenantal nomism," that is, "the conviction that status within the covenant (righteousness) is maintained by doing what the law requires (works of the law)."[6] "Living as a Jew" was differentiated from the lives of non-Jews by such boundary markers as circumcision, dietary practices, and Sabbath observance.

What we have to remember especially in reading Paul's hostile language about the law is that he did not reject the law for Jews. He did, however, separate salvation from the ethnic or national identity of Jews. It would not be by the adoption of this identity that Gentiles would share in the biblical promises of Israel but through their religious conversion and reorientation to the true God, what Paul calls "faith in Christ."

Seeing Merit

E. P. Sanders and others rejected the Christian assertion that by doing works Jews thought they would merit their own salvation. The theological principle that it is by God's grace that God saves is just as securely embedded in Second Temple Judaism as it would be in Christianity. As James Dunn argues, to abide by the law does not have to do with merit or earning salvation. The law was considered God's gift to Israel as the means for fulfilling Israel's covenant obligation to be faithful to God.[7] While Paul would have held that faith in Christ is necessary for both Jew and Gentile, he rejected the law only for Gentiles, not for Jews.

Seeing Women

While Paul's reference to Gentiles might appear specific, the meaning of the term is negative. It says only that a person is a non-Jew. The contrast between Jew and Gentile is uneven. One side of the contrast is a specific ethnic group; the other consists of everyone else. The phrase functions as a merism, a totality: there is nothing outside of Jew and non-Jew. It is a way of saying "everyone."

But, as we saw in the previous chapter, interpreters tend to use the term *Gentiles* as if it were an identifiable group like *Jews*. Moreover, they also tend to adopt the androcentrism of the biblical text, which uses Gentile as equivalent to *male*. A recent, not untypical article referred to Gentiles or Galatians several times in the first few pages. By linking the terms with circumcision the categories become masculine-specific. That some Gentiles were female disappears from view. It is impossible to raise questions about Galatian women in the analysis of this conflict if women are not there as part of the data for which the interpreter must account. Is it significant that Paul develops the notion of justification by faith in Galatians, that is, in the context of this particular conflict? This is a question raised by the article's author. Is it significant, we might add as a further question, that Paul develops the gender-neutral notion of justification by faith in a conflict that introduced a masculine-specific sign of membership? That question will not come up if the analysis of the conflict does not include all the players in the original context. The author uses Gentiles and Galatians in the following way; emphasis has been added to highlight the identification:

> Although scholars dispute exactly when Paul wrote Galatians and where the Galatian congregations were located, they agree that these congregations were composed of *gentiles*. It is also clear that when Paul preached the gospel to them, he did not

require the *Galatians to accept circumcision*, the sign of the eternal covenant God made with Abraham (Gen 17).

In requiring the *Galatians to adopt circumcision* and a Jewish way of life, the agitators may have argued in this fashion.

> Jesus was the Jewish Messiah, and you have done well to believe in him. Now you must perfect the faith you have embraced by having *yourselves circumcised* and adopting a Jewish way of life. After all, God made an eternal covenant with Abraham, the sign of which is circumcision. Moreover, the law pronounces a curse upon those who do not practice all of its prescriptions. The Messiah came so that even *gentiles* might live in accordance with God's law and become children of Abraham. Have *yourselves circumcised* then.

Therefore, there is no need for them to have *themselves circumcised* and adopt a Jewish way of life.

We dealt with the Galatian conflict in chapter 4. Here the point is that seeing women is crucial to analysis, but in order to see them we have to overcome the androcentrism of the biblical texts, which render women invisible, and then overcome the androcentrism of the history of interpretation, which has adopted the androcentrism of the text. In order that *Gentile* not be reduced to male only, we need to use *Gentile* in a gender-specific way to remind ourselves that it can mean either Gentile woman or Gentile man. Much rests on this hermeneutical connection.

QUESTIONS FOR UNDERSTANDING

Interpreting Paul's letters is the activity of raising and answering questions. Once we answer basic questions, like the ones below, we have a foundation for raising and answering more nuanced questions. The function of scholarly articles is to demonstrate how one has answered the questions relative to one's inquiry and to invite others to confirm one's understanding as correct. Scholarship becomes an interrelated set of judgments. We have sufficient evidence to say *X*, *Y*, and *Z*. Is the evidence sufficient for saying *A*, *B*, and *C*?

To Whom Is He Writing?

Is Paul writing to a community consisting of Jews, non-Jews, or both? With the exception of the Romans, a mixed community that he did not personally establish, Paul's letters are directed toward exclusively Gentile groups of women and men. He writes the letter with the expectation that the whole assembly will listen to it. His audience is the public assembly, not a set of private individuals. This is even the case with his letter to Philemon, a believer who remains a slave owner. In a situation that appears personal and the business of only one, Paul addresses the letter to several other individuals by name and the whole assembly that meets in this person's house.

Is He Writing Only to Men?

If the masculine language of a text corresponds to the historical situation from which it comes, Paul wrote only to men. They are "brothers" and "sons of God." But masculine-specific terms have long functioned as gender-inclusive, as *mankind* is said to do even today. The principle for Elisabeth Schüssler Fiorenza is this: "We can assume that New Testament androcentric language on the whole is inclusive of women until proven otherwise."[8] Modern translations apply this principle when they translate the masculine *brothers* with the gender-inclusive *brothers and sisters.*

Where Are They?

In the context of the first century, one is either in Palestine or one is in the Diaspora. This is another contrast in which one term is geographically specific (Palestine) while the other is abstract. Diaspora means "outside Israel," anywhere and everywhere one could be in the world.

The *where* also includes empire, not as an afterthought but as the foreground of Paul's missionary activity. There is nowhere he goes that is not subject to the control of the Roman Empire. We should keep in mind that this is the empire that killed Jesus and the empire in which Paul proclaims the crucified Jesus Lord and Savior.

It makes a difference to take into account the reality of empire as Paul's context, not least of all to ask how he survived so long with a message that undermined the power of the empire. All of the assemblies to which Paul writes are under the control of the Roman Empire. As we have seen, reading the hymn that Paul cites in his letter to the Philippians without thinking of the context as empire is different than thinking of empire as simply that which surrounds Paul. So, too, Paul's remark in 1 Corinthians that Christ will destroy every ruler, authority, and power (15:24–25) has little impact without the empire, but with it in mind as the political reality in which Paul writes, it is a truly shocking comment.

What Does Paul Address?

Paul responds to the problems, questions, and conflicts of assemblies he has founded. There is no dearth of problems. Some are ethical; for example, what to do if one is married to an unbelieving spouse, or what to do with a fellow believer who is engaging in scandalous behavior (such as being involved with his father's wife). Others are theological, such as the problem of members dying before Christ returns in judgment (raising the question: will they be raised up, too?). Belonging is a problem that raises dilemmas about factions (allegiance to one missionary or another), sharing equally in the liturgical meal (the rich leaving out the poor), or having one's values genuinely transformed by Christ (should the slaveholder free his slave?). 1 Corinthians may win the prize for the most problems of any community: a rough count yields at least thirteen different issues to which Paul responds. Romans is unusual in that it is difficult to know whether Paul is addressing their problems or his own. That he wants their help and support is clear enough, but he may be addressing internal difficulties of theirs, too.

Paul's advice and encouragement are often friendly, but at times he delivers biting criticism and condemnation. He is not above sarcasm, speaking meanly to people, or, as we saw in Galatians, even putting curses on his opponents. The problem of internal opponents transcends particular groups and times. Paul's interpretation of how Gentiles were to be included in the covenant of Israel was opposed by some Jesus followers from the beginning to the end of his career. Internal opposition was almost as difficult as the threats coming from outside the Jesus movement.

What Ideas Shape Paul's Response to These Assemblies?

As we saw in chapter 3, Paul's responses to these problems constitute "theology in the making." He had to bring his theological experience and mind to bear on the particular difficulties of believers and come up with answers to questions that he had not anticipated. His letters are not the product of leisurely reflection as much as they are the result of wrestling with these issues while working at his trade, traveling, or enduring imprisonment.

What Can We Expect to See in His Letters?

As we have seen, ten key concerns and themes recur in his correspondence:

1. *Eschatology*—the resurrection event is central to Paul's thinking. It signals the beginning of God's intervention in history against the domination of evil over creation. God's judgment of evildoers is ahead. Now is the time of repentance.
2. *Ethics*—believers are called to holiness, a morality shaped not only by a desire for the good but by the model of Jesus' suffering and self-sacrifice. The

moral transformation of Gentile women and men is empowered by the indwelling of the Holy Spirit.

3. *Spirit*—the giving of God's Spirit is an eschatological event. That Gentile women and men receive the gift of the Spirit through baptism and without the appropriation of the law as a way of living confirmed for Paul that his understanding of the condition for their inclusion in Israel's covenant—faith in Christ—was indeed correct.

4. *Truth of the gospel*—God's salvation is offered to Gentile women and men "as they are," that is, without becoming Jewish.

5. *Death of Christ*—God's resurrection of Jesus validated Jesus' life and death, removing the judgment of the law that death by crucifixion was the death of a sinner, an outsider to the law. Rather, Jesus' death atoned for the debt that Gentiles owed to God for their sin. As outsiders to the law, they now can accept God's offer of salvation through their faith in Christ.

6. *Obedience of Christ*—the obedience of Jesus, which brings life, is contrasted with the disobedience of Adam that brought sin into the world. Christ's being-for-others is the model for holiness.

7. *Risen Christ*—raised by God, Christ's resurrection signals also the promise of resurrection to believers. Lord and Savior, his power is cosmic, over all. God's raising of an outsider to the Law pointed to God's offer of salvation to the ultimate outsiders, Gentile women and men.

8. *Law*—Israel's obligation is to be faithful to God; the law is the means for meeting this obligation. It is a gift, not a burden. Paul did not dispute the value of the law for Jews but rejected the requirement that for Gentiles to be saved they must become Jews through full conversion and take on the way of living mandated by the Torah.

9. *Faith in Christ*—for Paul, this is the sole condition of membership that God has given to Gentile women and men as the means of accepting God's offer of salvation.

10. *Belonging to Christ*—one belongs to Christ, not to sin or to the world. Christ is the model of restored and redeemed humanity, and whoever belongs to Christ is a new creation. Christ has made Paul his own.

THE UNDISPUTED LETTERS

With these preliminary questions and themes in mind, we turn to the Pauline letters that are called undisputed and authentic. The undisputed letters have no question about their authorship. Questions have been raised about the other letters attributed to Paul in the New Testament, with the evidence pointing to writers other than Paul.

The undisputed letters show us a Paul whose initial experience with these different groups of people has shaped their subsequent relationships. He is on good terms with some assemblies; with others there is tension or reserve.[9]

Paul's casual descriptions of people reveal a movement that drew all sorts of people, some of whom Paul finds less than ideal. In Philippians, for example, he notes that many people proclaim Christ for many reasons, and of the four motives used only one is positive—from envy and rivalry, from goodwill, from selfish ambition (1:15–17). One letter may suggest something about another city or assembly. In 1 Thessalonians, for example, Paul writes that before coming to them, he and his missionary companions had been "shamefully mistreated at Philippi" (2:2). What happened in Philippi? In Paul's letter to the Philippians itself, with the exception of Paul's allusion to the (possible) persecution by Jews (3:2) and that the Philippians were undergoing the "same struggle that you saw I had" (1:30), we look in vain for a fuller account of this shameful event. But the remark in Thessalonians does put us on alert that there is some experience behind Paul's Philippian preaching that has an effect on his relationship with this city or assembly.

1 THESSALONIANS

Paul founded this assembly located in the capital city in Macedonia through his own preaching. He begins by identifying himself and other evangelists with whom he worked. The letter is from "Paul, Silvanus, and Timothy" (1:1). He addresses the letter to the Thessalonians, explicitly asking at the end of the letter that it be read aloud to the community (5:26). They are "in God," a holy community set apart by God.

Paul makes a clear distinction between God the Father and the Lord Jesus Christ (1:1). He does not identify Jesus as God but as the Messiah, the anointed one. This reference is not yet Trinitarian. Even if preexistent, which Paul may think he is, Jesus is not God but in some way subordinate to God. The full Trinitarian formulation will eliminate the subordination of the Son and add the Holy Spirit, but it is yet ahead. Paul refers separately to the power of the Holy Spirit in the context of their transformation in Christ (1:5).

Paul's tone in writing to the Thessalonians is easygoing. Having done nothing to insult or offend him, they are "very dear to us" (2:8). As evangelists, their conduct was "pure, upright, and blameless" (2:10).

Given Paul's comment that they have turned to God from idols (1:9), the recipients of the letter are Gentiles. Jews would not have to make such a turn. The many apocalyptic images and ideas suggest the main features of Paul's original preaching to them:

- God raised Jesus from the dead (1:10).
- The Son will return from heaven (1:10); the Lord will come (4:15).
- Jesus will save us from the wrath that is coming (1:10, 2:16).
- The dead will rise first (4:16).
- The living will be caught up in the clouds with the Lord (4:17).
- Christ died for us so that we may live with him (5:10).

The political claims of the Roman Empire's Pax Romana, its claims to have achieved peace and security, were challenged by Paul's dramatic apocalyptic image of the future "day of the Lord":

> For you yourselves know very well that the day of the Lord will
> come like a thief in the night. When they say: "There is peace
> and security," then sudden destruction will come upon them,
> as labor pains come upon a pregnant woman, and there will be
> no escape! (5:3)

Paul's statement is striking in its clear reference to the destruction of imperial powers. Christ is not above the political order or unconnected to it but poses a direct challenge to its existence. Unlike the destruction predicted for the empire, Christ "rescues us from the wrath to come" (1:10). The day of the Lord will be deliverance for followers (4:13–18).

Paul expresses relief that Timothy found them still with faith (3:2). He had preached to them despite great opposition (2:2). Now he is worried that continued opposition and persecution might diminish their commitment. Happily, though, by sending Timothy he has now been assured that their commitment has held fast.

One of the assembly's difficulties is the sexual behavior of some of its members (4:3–8). Paul reminds them that they have learned from him how they ought to live (4:1). The will of God for them is ethical. He instructs them to refrain from improper sexual relations. He constructs a "Gentile ethics" from two commands of the Hebrew Bible, appealing to them to love one another (3:12, 4:9; cf. Lev 19:18) and to do the good. Do not repay "evil for evil, but always seek to do good to one another and to all" (5:15; cf. Amos 5:14–15), repeating the principle a few lines down: "hold fast to what is good; abstain from every form of evil" (5:21).

The central problem of the Thessalonians, however, is directly connected with the eschatological dimension of Paul's preaching. They accepted the idea that the end time had begun with the resurrection of Jesus and that by belonging to Jesus Christ, they would share his resurrection. From Paul they were led to believe that Jesus would return soon in judgment. Only those who belonged to Christ would share in the general resurrection.

What the members of this assembly did not expect was for anyone in their group to die before Christ's return. But now members had died and Christ had not yet returned. Their pressing question was whether those who had died would still share in Christ's resurrected life. Paul assured them that the dead would still share in the benefits of the assembly (4:14). Even in death they were still members of the assembly—the real worry of the assembly. Before the living share the fruits of Christ's resurrection, those who have died will be called forth to join him:

> For since we believe that Jesus died and rose again, even so, through Jesus, God will bring with him those who have died. For this we declare to you by the word of the Lord, that we who are alive, who are left until the coming of the Lord, will by no means precede those who have died. For the Lord himself, with a cry of command, with the archangel's call and with the sound of God's trumpet, will descend from heaven, and the dead in Christ will rise first. Then we who are alive, who are left, will be caught up in the clouds together with them to meet the Lord in the air; and so we will be with the Lord forever.

Fundamentalists expect Paul's dramatic images to become a reality for them in the future. But the effort Paul puts into this vivid scene is for one purpose: to convince those still alive among the Thessalonians that belonging to the *ekklēsia* does not end with death. The benefit it offers to its members is salvation. Those who have died are destined not for God's wrath but, through Jesus Christ, still for God's salvation. They, too, will live with Christ (5:9–10).

PHILIPPIANS

Paul calls the members of the Philippian church "saints." His reference to "bishops and deacons" is, in the view of some, better translated "overseers and helpers" because the prior terms denote offices that had not yet developed. Again Paul offers grace and peace but from God the father and the Lord Jesus Christ. Reference to the Spirit comes in a few lines. He writes to them as citizens of heaven (3:20), using the word *ekklēsia*, employed for the gathering of citizens in the Greek city.

Paul's first reason for writing was to tell the Philippians that he was sending Epaphroditus back to them. Epaphroditus brought Paul gifts from the Philippian assembly to meet his needs while imprisoned. He had become quite ill while with Paul. Paul's relationship with this assembly is close. He expresses thanks for the care they have given to him in the past and now when he is in prison (4:14). No church has stood with him as they have (4:15). You "hold me in your heart," he writes to them (1:7). He has hopes for being released: "I trust in the Lord that I will also come soon" (2:24). He makes no reference to difficulties in Philippi that he alludes to in Thessalonians: "we had . . . been shamefully mistreated in Philippi" (1 Thess 2:2).

Paul's apocalyptic horizon is in evidence in this letter, as it was in 1 Thessalonians. It is complemented by the language of participation with Christ. They await the day of Jesus Christ (1:6, 1:10, 2:16). The saints are "in Christ Jesus" (1:1). Paul is "living in Christ" (1:21). In this in-between time, the challenge is ethical. Paul hopes that on the "day of Christ" they will be shown to be "blameless and innocent" (1:15).

With Epaphroditus's return, Paul writes also to con-front the disharmony and disunity in the assembly. At least one cause is the alienation between Eudia and Syntyche, two women leaders—evangelists—who apparently have had some big falling out (4:2–3). Paul urges them to be "of the same mind" (4:2). This may be the cause of fac-tions within the assembly. As in other places, Paul deals with the presence of other Jesus evangelists whose mes-sage to the believers in this assembly is different than Paul's own. He questions their motives (1:15–18). He takes par-ticularly hostile aim at evangelists who must have insisted that belonging to Israel's covenant required circumcision for men and Torah observance. His reference to them is insulting: "Beware of the dogs, beware of the evil workers, beware of those who mutilate the flesh!" (3:2).

In opposing disharmony in the community, Paul appeals to the Philippians to "make [his] joy complete: be of the same mind, having the same love, being in full accord and of one mind" (2:1). He encourages them to imitate him and what they have "heard and seen in me" (4:9). With unity an ideal, he appeals to the model of Christ for its meaning: "Let the same mind be in you that was in Christ" (2:5). Here Paul inserts an early Christian hymn (2:6–11) that portrays Christ in contrast to the values of the ancient world. Instead of seeking honor and high status as do the elites, from a preexistent state with God—no higher place of honor could be conceived—Christ took the form of a slave, the lowest of the low in the social order (2:7). The very idea of appropriating the identity of a nonperson would have been insulting to an elite in Paul's world. In contrast to Adam's disobedience, Christ's obedience was unrestricted, opening him even to death.

As we have seen, the Christ hymn Paul cites is striking if it is read with the background of the empire brought into focus. Such a proclamation would be suspect indeed:

> Therefore God also highly exalted him and gave him the name that is above every name, so that at the name of Jesus every knee should bend, in heaven and on earth and under the earth, and every tongue should confess that Jesus Christ is Lord, to the glory of God the Father. (2:9–11)

The hymn appropriates what would normally be said only of the emperor, placing these claims under the cosmic patronage of God the Father for Jesus.

That this proclamation is about a man crucified by the empire makes it all the more striking. To call Jesus Lord challenged and subverted the lordship of the emperor. The proclamation of the hymn is a form of resistance strategy against the empire. It decentered and destabilized the empire's claim to absolute power.[10] In a further distancing of themselves from the empire, Paul emphasizes that they belong to Christ; their "citizenship is in heaven" (3:20). If they belong there, they are foreigners here. The "day

of Christ" (2:16) is the end of this present evil age and
the beginning of a new age. The beginning of God's reign
implies the end of Rome's reign. Power is given to Christ
"to make all things subject to himself" (3:21). They are to
be "blameless and innocent" in the "midst of a crooked
and perverse generation" (2:15). God's wrath will con-
sume others: "Their end is their destruction; their god is
the belly; and they glory in their shame; their minds are set
on earthly things" (3:19).

PHILEMON

Paul wrote this brief letter with Timothy, his fellow evangelist. While he uses "prisoner of Christ" as a metaphor,
Paul was an actual prisoner, too. Where he was confined
is not known. But a slave belonging to a member of the
Philippian assembly, Philemon, turned up in this prison
with Paul. Paul wrote to Philemon about Onesimus, his
slave, but he did not intend the letter to remain private.
The letter is addressed to two others by name, Apphia and
Archippus, and to the whole assembly. As we have seen in
other letters, Paul extends a greeting of grace and peace
from God the Father and the Lord Jesus Christ. This letter,
however, has no reference to the Holy Spirit.

That Paul would know slave owners and slaves would
not have been unusual. Any reference to someone that he
knew as a "head of household" was likely to be the owner
of slaves. The Roman Empire was a slave state. Huge numbers of people became slaves from warfare, or from within
the Roman Empire, from failed insurrections. Slaves did
work of all kinds—fields, mines, business, and domestic.

By law, Philemon would have had unrestricted power over Onesimus, including the freedom to beat him to death for any perceived infraction. Running away was punishable by death. Paul's reference to Onesimus's wronging Philemon, saying, "[if he] owes you anything, charge that to my account" (1:17), suggests the slave stole something—food, perhaps—on the way out.

As the baptism fragment Paul integrates at Galatians 3:28 states that "there is no longer slave or free," Philemon, a slave owner, has joined a religious group that explicitly rejects the kind of domination that he holds over his slave. It is likely that he has more than one. Paul appeals to him as one who has entered a new social reality with new values and expectations. The construction of the letter is careful. The effectiveness of Paul's rhetoric gives rise to the image of a noose around Philemon's neck with sharp tugs being given to it periodically. The tugs are at these points:

- Paul addresses the letter to the whole assembly (1:1).
- He prays that Philemon's faith "become effective" (1:6).
- He sends with Onesimus "my very heart" (1:12).
- He asks that Philemon accept Onesimus "as a brother" (1:16).
- He hopes Philemon will accept Onesimus back "as more than a slave" (1:15).
- Paul offers to repay anything Onesimus owes Philemon (1:18).
- Philemon owes his very self to Paul (1:19).

- Paul knows that Philemon will do "even more than I say" (1:21).
- Paul tells Philemon to prepare a guest room, because he is coming (1:23).

Commentators in the tradition have professed uncertainty about what Paul wants Philemon to do. What Paul says, though, seems transparent. Their uncertainty may have had more to do with the church's legitimation of slavery until the late nineteenth century and an unwillingness to undermine slave owners than with the letter itself. Paul asserts that with his authority he could command Philemon to do his duty and then makes the first sharp tug: he is sending Onesimus back, "that is, my own heart" (1:12). A further tug comes when Paul says "welcome him as you would welcome me" (1:17). Welcoming Onesimus as like Paul would be to welcome him as a free person. Paul's request that Philemon welcome Onesimus back "no longer as a slave but more than a slave, a beloved brother" need not be interpreted as metaphorical but as a subtle way of asking for Onesimus's manumission. If he is like a brother to Philemon, Onesimus's status would be not only free but presumably elite. Paul has left Philemon's duty unnamed (1:8), asserting later that he is confident of Philemon's obedience (1:21). He leaves the nature of Philemon's obedience unnamed, too. But both are clear. Philemon is to be obedient to Christ and to the values he has professed upon entering the community. Freeing Onesimus is his one duty.

The matter with which Paul deals—perhaps a master with a runaway slave or perhaps a slave loaned to Paul—

would seem to be private; but Paul addresses the letter to the whole assembly, signaling that he considers the problem to be a communal one. It is not that others will decide Onesimus's fate but that with Philemon they are part of this new social reality created through different relationships and values. They belong to Christ, including Onesimus. He no longer belongs to Philemon. Paul's frequent tugs at the noose indicate his desire that Philemon make his baptismal profession real by freeing Onesimus.

By identifying Onesimus with himself, Paul has made it virtually impossible for Philemon to think of Onesimus simply as a disobedient slave. Clearly Philemon did not take his baptismal profession literally or he would have rejected his own privilege as a slave owner. Paul now makes himself the baptismal profession: what Philemon does to Onesimus, he does to Paul, to whom, Paul says so casually, Philemon owes his very self. Presumably Paul means that by his preaching and Philemon's subsequent conversion, Paul provided Philemon with the means of his salvation. He tugs sharply at the noose when he announces he is coming. No longer will he consider the relationship between Onesimus and Philemon from a distance. Paul signs off with one final tug—naming those with him who extend their greetings, who know what Paul has asked of Philemon: Epaphras, Mark, Aristarchus, Demas, and Luke (1:23).

Like all the conflicts Paul addresses in his letters, we do not know the results of his letter to Philemon. Did Paul's letter cause Philemon difficulties with other members of their assembly? Did Philemon free Onesimus?

This letter, like those of Paul to the Thessalonians and to the Philippians, is ultimately about belonging. To whom does Onesimus belong? To whom does Philemon belong? In Philemon's world, Onesimus is a nonperson. But to Paul, and in the age that will replace this evil age, Onesimus is a person with the dignity God has given human beings. He should not be owned by Philemon but accepted by him as a brother, as an equal.

1 AND 2 CORINTHIANS

Paul's introduction to the Jesus followers in the major urban center of Corinth coincided with the exile of Jews from Rome by Claudius (49 C.E.) and the arrival in Corinth of a couple, Prisca and Aquila, who were already engaged in missionary work with the Corinthians. Their house-church was the first assembly in Corinth. Paul worked with them in their shared profession of tent making and in proclaiming Jesus as the Messiah (Acts 18:1–5). By the time Paul is writing this letter, Prisca and Aquila have moved to Ephesus, where they are again with Paul (16:19).

Perhaps because of the range of issues about which he intends to give instruction, Paul begins his first letter with a clear designation of his authority as an apostle. He is called by the will of God (1:1). He extends the grace and peace of God the Father and the Lord Jesus Christ to the saints in Corinth from himself and Sosthenes (1:1).

The several Corinthian assemblies to whom Paul writes have the dubious honor of having the most problems of any community to which he wrote. They include:

- Divisions; factions
- Exclusionary behavior of members at liturgical meals

- Status distinctions in spirituality
- Sexual immorality
- Court suits against one another
- Continued participation in other religious rites
- Questions about marriage, divorce, celibacy

All of these problems touch upon a basic one of belonging. Believers do not belong to the world or the empire. They do not belong to one evangelist or another. They do not belong because they have this gift or that. They belong to Christ. This is what has turned them to the true God of Israel, to engage in a life of holiness, to turn from sin to righteousness. This is what has made them a new creation.

Should the man living with his father's wife be allowed to continue to belong? Do those who have wisdom, who think of themselves as more mature or perfect spiritually, belong more than those who are less mature? Do disagreements among members belong within the community instead of courts outside the assembly? Can one belong to the Jesus assembly and still eat meat sacrificed in pagan temples?

Are there spiritual practices that disrupt rather than contribute to harmony? Paul engages in a long discussion about the gift of tongues, cautioning those who have it not to think it is more important than other gifts. The community should not forbid speaking in tongues, but Paul cautions that "all things should be done decently and in order" (14:40).

Paul emphasizes that the Corinthian believers belong to Christ, and Christ belongs to God (3:23). He does not believe in status differences nor gender differences. They are all to imitate him (11:1).

The underlying eschatology of Paul's worldview is evident in the way he addresses each of these problems. It is clearly evident in his opinion of what they should do with the man and his mother-in-law:

> When you are assembled, and my spirit is present with the power of our Lord Jesus Christ, you are to hand this man over to Satan for the destruction of his flesh, so that his spirit may be saved in the day of the Lord. (5:4–5)

Paul's eschatological hopes are ethical. He hopes they will "be blameless on the day of the Lord Jesus Christ" (1:8). He expects them to reject practices from their old lives and to live according to new values. Paul is anxious that the Corinthian believers will not find themselves in the right place when Christ returns. He describes what some of them used to be: fornicators, idolaters, thieves, male prostitutes (6:9). He encourages them to "drive out the wicked person from among you" (5:13).

Leander Keck explains Paul's way of thinking in terms of "structures of existence" in which one participates. The transfer from what the Corinthians used to be to what they became is a transfer in structures. "Paul's gospel announces that emancipation from one structure is possible because participation in another is available."[11] Christ, the eschatological event, is a new structure of existence. Believers have transferred to Christ from sin as a structure of existence in which they participate. They are a new creation in this structure of existence.

The assembly is the body of Christ. Paul uses the image of the body to reinforce the Gentiles' call to holiness as well as his appeal for unity among them. Inasmuch as the body of Christ is holy, the body of the individual member should be, too. The image of the body functions for the eschatological assembly in the way that the Torah has for the people of Israel: as the boundary between inside and out. Outside is pagan culture and nonbelievers. Their body is the temple of the Holy Spirit (6:19). Those who belong to Christ will be alive in Christ when the end comes (15:23). He is the first fruits of a resurrected new humanity (15:20).

Because the Gentile believers have not appropriated the Jewish law, Paul cannot draw on the Torah for the specific moral direction he wishes to give to them. Instead, he appeals to their reception of the Spirit as the source of their moral transformation. They are to live in the Spirit. The chief gift of the Spirit is love (13:1–13). "Let all you do be done in love" (16:14). He ends with a short eschatological prayer: "Our Lord, come!" (16:21).

Paul's focus is theocentric—it is God who raised Jesus from the dead—but also christological—it is Christ who reveals God. Moreover, he proclaims the crucified Jesus (1:23), the one killed by imperial powers. But God's raising Jesus shows this power to be an illusion. Jesus is Lord and Son of God, *kyrios* and *divi filius*, titles both used by emperors (12:3, 1:9). When one remembers that the Roman Empire is still very much in power during Paul's ministry, his reference to the future time of judgment seems extraordinarily risky:

> Then comes the end, when he hands over the kingdom to God the Father, after he has destroyed every ruler and every authority and power. (15:24)

Christ's obedience replaces Adam's disobedience (15:21–22). It is the prototype for the ethical lives of believers. For Christ, obedience led to death. His death is atoning; it reconciles human beings with God (15:3). The power of the cross is power to take away sin (1:17).

More significant even than its atoning meaning is Paul's understanding of Jesus' death as something believers participate in. They share in his death. This is the way in which one dies to sin and belongs to God.[12] They come into the assembly through baptism, which symbolizes their dying with Christ. The church is the body of Christ.

Paul's second letter to the Corinthians is considered by many scholars to be a composite of several letters. The tone of the letter changes abruptly in several places, joyful in one place, suddenly somber in another. These must have been several letters exchanged between Paul and the Corinthian assemblies (5:9). He learns through a visit of Timothy to Corinth that other Jesus evangelists have been preaching in these communities and have directly opposed his gospel. He indicates that his upcoming visit will be his third visit. He refers polemically to these opposing evangelists as false apostles (11:3) and superapostles (2 Cor 11:5, 12:11).

When he visited the Corinthians again, things did not go well. Paul refers to a "painful visit" (2:1). One of the members apparently offended him. He indicates that he wrote to them to tell them of his love for them but out of "much distress and anguish of heart and with many tears" (2:4). He indicates in this letter that there are no restrictions on his affections for them but there are restrictions on their part (6:12). He defends himself: "We have wronged no one, we have taken advantage of no one" (7:2), criticisms that may have been made of him and to which he is responding. He refers either to another letter or this one written in much distress, saying that he was sorry that he had grieved them with his letter. He appeals to belonging to Christ as the criterion for self-evaluation (10:7). He calls on them to examine themselves. He does not develop the theme of the body of Christ as he did in the first letter but reminds them that "Christ is in you" (13:5).

Paul instead develops the theme of participation in Christ in this second letter, saying, "So if anyone is in Christ, there is a new creation" (5:17). The restoration of creation distorted by sin is underway. Christ's death has atoned for sin. God has "reconciled us to himself through Christ," and Paul's ministry is reconciliation (5:18).

This letter ends with the three divine names, instead of the two in other letters: "The grace of the Lord Jesus Christ, the love of God, and the communion of the Holy Spirit be with all of you" (13:13).

GALATIANS

We dealt with the Galatian conflict in chapter 4. However, the main elements of the letter are as follows. The salutation of Galatians has the strongest defense of Paul's apostleship of all the letters. His authority comes from God, not from human authorities (Gal 1:1). The Jerusalem apostles are likely those being excluded as influential. He gives a brief account of his life, first as persecutor of the Jesus followers and then, after a mystical experience, as a follower himself and a missionary (1:13–24).

Paul tells then of his visit to Jerusalem to negotiate with the apostles there. He left with an agreement that it was right for him to continue his Diaspora mission to the Gentiles as he had been doing (2:1–10). The high point is the second story, that of Peter's hypocrisy in Antioch. Paul calls him a hypocrite because he first shared table fellowship with Gentiles but then backed off when the Torahobservant Jesus followers came to Antioch (2:11–14). This story serves as a backdrop to what is happening now in the Galatian assemblies.

The Jerusalem disciples have arrived again—it could be the same ones, but given the time frame they are probably different. Paul asks rhetorically, "Who has bewitched you?" (3:1). He points to the reception of the Spirit as validation of his position on the inclusion of Gentile women and men in Israel's covenant (3:2). All are children of God; there are no more separate and unequal spheres (3:26–29). He discusses the role of the law and constructs the allegory of Sarah and Hagar, the free woman and the slave woman (4:21–31).

Paul proclaims their freedom (5:1) and threatens Galatian men who are considering circumcision with cutting themselves off from Christ if they do so (5:4). His ethics of the Spirit replaces the Torah as the generating power of moral transformation for Gentiles. Live by the Spirit; the fruits of the Spirit are manifest first in love of neighbor (5:16–21). By uniting themselves with Jesus in his death, they will also be united with him in his resurrection. But what is important now is that the old self was crucified with him so that the power of sin might be overcome (Rom 6:5–6).

Throughout the tradition, commentators have stressed that at the heart of the Galatian conflict is the claim of equality. The "truth of the Gospel" for Paul was that Gentiles were now to be included in Israel's covenant of salvation with Jews. Those arguing for the equality of Gentiles with Jews were themselves Gentiles.

By the second century, Jesus followers were predominantly non-Jewish, making the question of self-identity acute. They were Gentiles, but they counted the Hebrew scriptures as their own. Their worship and offices were patterned after those of the synagogue, and their interpretation of the atoning death of Jesus flowed from the practice of offering sacrifices in the Temple.

John Pawlikowski writes that the early Christians who asked the question, "Who are we?" answered it by saying, "We have replaced them." This began the supersessionist tradition, which I discuss in chapter 7.

Interpretation of the Galatian conflict requires discarding some long-standing assumptions. First among these is the assertion that Paul rejected Judaism and converted from Judaism to Christianity. Second is the claim that Paul rejected the law and adopted a superior spirituality of faith. Third is a conception of justification that keeps it an individual reality rather than one that has to do with the social reality of the assembly. Fourth is the perception of the Palestinian evangelists as engaged in imposing a legalistic and hypocritical spirituality onto the Galatians.

Scholars under the umbrella term *new perspective* have emphasized and criticized the supersessionist tendency of the above assumptions and stressed the need to see the social dimensions of the conflict over circumcision.[13] The conflict is over membership in the eschatological Israel. As E. P. Sanders put it: How are Gentiles to come in and stay in?

Paul and his challengers shared an eschatological horizon, namely:

- That the resurrection of Jesus signaled to both Paul and the other evangelists that God was beginning the end time.
- That if the end time was beginning, Israel's function of being a light to the world was fulfilled and now Gentiles would join Israel's covenant of salvation and worship the true God.
- That the creation distorted by sin was now being restored by Christ's redemption.

Paul parted ways with his fellow evangelists on these points which he held and they disputed:

- That the law, which designated a crucified man a sinner and thus an outsider to the law (Deut 21:23), was no longer normative in light of God's resurrection of this crucified man.
- That Gentiles, as outsiders to the law, were validated by God's offer of salvation to them.
- That God's offer to Gentile women and men came without the requirement to observe the law.
- That the gift of the Spirit received by Gentiles through baptism was a validation of Paul's gospel.

In the existing gender-inclusive and emancipated communities, the insistence on a male-specific sign of full membership would raise a red flag.[14] If the Palestinian evangelists were offended that Peter was eating with Gentiles, was it because that meant he was eating with Gentile women? If these assemblies became structured by the Torah—especially as interpreted by theologically conservative men from Jerusalem—they would reflect the patriarchal world around them, starting with male privilege.

Commentators from the tradition were right that Paul's letter to the Galatians was about equality. Their question was whether these other evangelists came to oppose Gentile men being part of the covenant without the sign of full membership. They overlooked the full data: the assemblies included women, and acceptance of circumcision would have affected them, too. Circumcision signals both religious and gender privilege.

In his response, Paul did not explicitly address the gender implications of the demand for circumcision. But he did reinforce the gender inclusiveness of membership:

- Both women and men come in through faith in Christ.
- Both are initiated through baptism.
- Both receive the gift of the Spirit.
- Both can receive the gift of being apostles, evangelists, prophets, and teachers.
- Both are heirs of Abraham.
- Both belong to Christ.

This letter, like Paul's others, is about belonging. Who belongs to the assembly? How? We know nothing about what happened in these communities after Paul's letter. Did they remain faithful to Paul's gospel? Did they accept the interpretation of the men from James? Did the conflict between evangelists break up the assemblies completely? We will see in the discussion of the disputed letters in chapter 6 how this change was attempted without circumcision.

The baptismal confession cited by Paul in Galatians 3:28 shows three fundamental distinctions within the social order. For the boundaries of each pair to be "no longer" means that the privilege associated with the superior part of the pair has been eliminated. There is no longer religious privilege, class privilege, or gender privilege in the eschatological community. The distinctions have been relativized. While the privileged person in the pair was presumed to have access or status before God that the nonprivileged one did not have, according to this confession such was no longer the case. The language of the baptismal confession implies, writes James Dunn, "a radically reshaped social world as viewed from a Christian perspective."[15] To recall our theme of belonging, each member of the assembly belongs fully to Christ; each belongs fully to the *ekklēsia*. While Dunn adverts to gender in saying that Paul would not have allowed gender to constitute a barrier against service to the gospel, he does not advert to the fact that privilege would be reintroduced by a gendered sign of membership, as the circumcision preachers advocated.

ROMANS

Considered the most systematic of all his letters, Paul's letter to the Romans is dated around 58 C.E., the last he wrote. He longs to see them, Paul tells the Roman believers. He will come after he delivers a collection to Jerusalem and on his way to Spain (15:24). When he did arrive in Rome, however, it would be in the chains of a prisoner.

Unlike Paul's other letters, Romans is written to a community that Paul did not establish and had not even visited. It is likely there were several groups meeting in house and tenement churches, as Peter Lampe calls them. The name of the one responsible for preaching the Gospel there and starting these communities is lost to historical memory. The community was mixed, Jews and Gentiles, and inclusive, women and men.

Romans 16 does preserve from historical memory, however, some of the names of the many people engaged in the ministry and life of the Jesus movement.[16] The bearer of Paul's letter is Phoebe, whom Paul identifies as a deacon of the assembly at Cenchreae, and a benefactor to many, including Paul (16:1–2). He sends greetings to a number of people he knows in Rome.

These greetings are a particularly valuable source of knowledge for women's participation and leadership in the Jesus assemblies. "Greet Prisca and Aquila, who work with me in Christ Jesus" (16:3). Paul greets Mary, "who has worked very hard among you" (16:6), a euphemism meaning evangelist or missionary, and several others. "Greet Andronicus and Junia, my relatives who were in prison with me, they are prominent among the apostles, and they were in Christ before me" (16:7) Junia, a feminine name, became Junias, a masculine name, in the tradition. How and why is unknown; it could have been simply a copying mistake. But it is not totally unthinkable that a conscientious scribe changed the noun from its feminine form to a masculine one because of his assumption that a woman could not have been an apostle.

As in his other letters, Paul addresses a number of problems in Romans, offers unsolicited ethical direction, and issues various admonitions about disharmony, tensions between the "strong" and the "weak," those who cause dissensions and offenses, and other difficulties.

But whose problem is central? Paul's or the Romans'? The question of why Paul wrote to the Romans remains an open one.[17] Three hypotheses are advanced.

Roman Exile Hypothesis

This argument presumes the problem to which Paul responds is on the side of the Romans.[18]

In 49 C.E. the Roman emperor Claudius expelled Jews from Rome for an uprising and fight over "Christus." The name surely refers to Jesus as the Messiah, in Greek "Christ." The fight was between messianic Jews who proclaimed Christ as God's anointed one and Jews who rejected this claim. With Jewish Jesus followers exiled from Rome, the Jesus assembly became exclusively Gentile women and men.[19]

Jewish Jesus followers returned to Rome under an edict of the Emperor Nero in 54 C.E. The conflicts to which Paul alludes in this letter suggest that their return was not wholeheartedly welcomed or comfortably accommodated by the Gentile women and men who had remained in the community for the five years. Paul addressed divisions in the Roman community. He encouraged the basic condition for belonging, that is, genuine acceptance of the other.

Jerusalem Crisis Hypothesis

This argument puts the problem on Paul's side. As part of an agreement he had made with the Jerusalem leaders, Paul took up a collection among his Gentile believers for the poor in the Jerusalem assembly (Gal 2:10; Rom 15:25). Paul is anxious about this upcoming visit to Jerusalem. Will the collection be accepted? He appealed to the Roman assembly for their support. In fact, when he did take the collection to Jerusalem, it was refused. Jerusalem would be no more welcoming of Paul than of Jesus.

Spanish Mission Hypothesis

Yet a third argument keeps the problem on Paul's side. It views the purpose of the letter as Paul's desire to extend his mission into Spain (15:24). He writes to the house and tenement churches in Rome for their support.[20]

Romans begins with an extended salutation in which Paul grounds his apostleship in a prophetic call, declares he belongs to Christ as a servant—as do the Romans—and proclaims the resurrection. He grounds the identity of the Son in the line of David and attributes Jesus' title of Son of God to the "spirit of holiness," that is, to God's Spirit. As he does of his own converts, he calls the Romans saints, holy ones.

Paul begins by praising their faith. He laments that he had hoped to visit them but had not been able to do so (1:11–12). He describes the gospel he has wanted to proclaim to them:

> For I am not ashamed of the gospel; it is the power of God for salvation to everyone who has faith, to the Jew first and also the Greek. For in it the righteousness of God is revealed through faith, for faith; as it is written, "The one who is righteous will live by faith." (1:17)

Much of Paul's theology and worldview is packed into these two sentences. First, the gospel is not just for insiders to the covenant but also for outsiders. The inclusion of Gentiles in Israel's covenant was at the heart of Paul's ministry. His prophetic call was to preach to the Gentiles. For both Jews and Gentiles, the condition for acceptance of salvation was faith. In contrast to a routine interpretation in the tradition, however, Paul did not reject the use of the law for Jews. It constituted a distinctive way of life. Torah observance would remain a means of covenant fidelity for them. But for both Jew and Gentile, confession of Jesus was necessary: "Everyone who calls on the name of the Lord shall be saved" (10:13).

Paul's language is characteristically apocalyptic: "the wrath of God" will oppose all ungodliness and wickedness (1:18). He writes, "The God of Peace will shortly crush Satan under your feet." Believers will be saved from God's wrath through Jesus (5:9). Salvation requires one confession: "If you confess with your lips that Jesus is Lord and believe in your heart that God raised him from the dead, you will be saved" (10:9).

Paul describes a fallen world, distorted by failing to honor God, whose existence is made clear through the things he has made, and by disordered passions and debased minds that choose to do evil rather than good (1:18). Just as God shows no partiality in his offer of salvation, so, too, there will be no partiality in punishment for sin (2:11). In this context, the place of the Jew and Gentile is the same: both are under the power of sin (3:9).

Paul's Christology is summed up in this reality: all are in need of redemption because all are under the power of sin. A poignant moment of self-revelation captures the human dilemma for Paul:

> I do not understand my own actions. For I do not do what I want, but I do the very thing I hate. Now if I do what I do not want, I agree that the law is good. But in fact it is no longer I that do it, but sin that dwells within me. For I know that nothing good dwells within me, that is, in my flesh. I can will what is right, but I cannot do it. For I do not do the good I want, but the evil I do not want is what I do. (7:15–19)

What hope is there if this is the human dilemma? Believers have been rescued by Christ and freed from bondage to sin (8:1–2). This is God's remedy for restoring creation from the distortion sin has caused. Through baptism believers share Christ's death and through being united to him share in the promise of his resurrection as well (6:4–5): "But if we have died with Christ, we believe we will also live with him" (6:8).

Paul's theology of redemption draws on the notion of sin as debt and Christ's death as an expiation—payment—of this debt. The familiar idea of blood sacrifice as atonement for sin is extended to the death of Jesus. It is redemptive. It brings humankind back to God, reconciles humankind with God. The means of salvation is faith in Christ: "[Sinners] are justified freely by [God's] grace through the redemption in Christ Jesus, whom God set forth as an expiation, through faith, by his blood" (3:24).

This news is especially relevant for those outside the covenant: "Christ died for the ungodly" (5:6). His obedience has led to "justification and life for all," overcoming death as the effect of Adam's disobedience (5:17–18).

God's validation—resurrection—of a crucified man said to Paul that the law, which condemned Jesus as a sinner, was no longer normative. Jesus was not a sinner if he was validated by God. The law no longer defined the boundaries of salvation. The good news that Paul proclaimed was God's offer of salvation for all. What was the exclusive right of Jews prior to the death of Jesus was now an inclusive offer. "Gentiles" did not refer to one group among many but together with "Jews" it meant everyone. There was no one outside of Jew and non-Jew. The offer of salvation was open and the status of Jew and Gentile was now equal: "there is no distinction between Jew and Greek: the same Lord is Lord of all and is generous to all who call on him" (10:12).

Paul worries about the fact that all of Israel has not responded to this proclamation with enthusiasm. He speculates that their stumbling has been the means of Gentile salvation, which in turn will make them jealous and facilitate their acceptance of the message (11:11–14). He cautions Gentiles in the Roman assemblies not to be conceited about their inclusion (11:20). Jews are still God's beloved, "for the gifts and the calling of God are irrevocable" (11:29).

Paul reaches back to Abraham as the prototype of one who has faith (4:11). All humankind will be saved through faith. Persons are now justified "by faith apart from works prescribed by the law" (3:28). God "reckons righteousness apart from works" (4:6). But it is also God's impartial righteousness that has been revealed:

> But now apart from the law, the righteousness of God has been disclosed, and is attested by the law and prophets, the righteousness of God through faith in Jesus Christ for all who believe. (3:21–22)

In this eschatological time initiated by Christ's resurrection, faith is the condition for being in right relation with God. The indwelling of divine presence confirms this condition as sufficient. The gift of the Spirit empowers believers in moral living: "God's love has been poured into our hearts through the Holy Spirit that has been given to us" (5:5). Those who have the Spirit belong to Christ (8:9). It is the source of moral transformation, generating the power for living rightly. Gifts of the Spirit ground the charismatic equality of the community: "all who are led by the Spirit of God are children of God" (8:14).

Paul draws upon the image of the body of Christ for his ethical direction. While they have different gifts, they are one body and individually members of one another (12:5).

He appeals to them to "let love be genuine; hate what is evil, hold fast to what is good" (12:9).

QUESTIONS FOR
REFLECTION AND DISCUSSION

1. How do Paul's letters function? In general, to what is Paul responding in each? What is an example of something we should not assume, "not see," when reading one of his letters?
2. The term *polemical* has come up several times. Give an example of polemical language found in Paul and what he is doing in talking this way.
3. Christians have used *works* with regard to Judaism in a very negative way. How are the meanings of works developed in the Christian tradition and works as the term would have been understood in the first century (recovered by Sanders and Dunn)?
4. Take one of the New Testament letters of Paul to read. Read about it in *Encountering Paul.* Write the letter that Paul could have received from someone in that assembly to which he is responding in his own. Describe the problems, questions, and conflicts from the point of view of someone in the community.

6

Disputed Letters

In his letter to the Galatians, Paul writes: "For freedom Christ has set us free. Stand firm, therefore, and do not submit again to a yoke of slavery" (Gal 5:1). In 1 Corinthians he writes: "Were you a slave when called? Do not be concerned about it. . . . In whatever condition you were called, brothers and sisters, there remain with God" (1 Cor 7:21, 24).

From what does he think Christ has freed human beings? Where is freedom when he advocates that the slave not be concerned about his or her bondage? Both Galatians and 1 Corinthians were written by Paul, but the views they express are so different that they seem not to originate in the same writer. Does Paul envision redemption with freedom? If so, how can he ask people to conform to the oppressive structures of the world? How does he do both?

This dilemma grows more complex when we look at Paul's letters as a whole. Thirteen letters are attributed to him in the New Testament. For seven letters there is every reason to think he wrote them and no reason to think he did not. Written in the mid-first century C.E., the undisputed letters are 1 Thessalonians, Philemon, Philippians, 1 and 2 Corinthians, Galatians, and Romans. These authentic letters were written in response to problems, questions, and conflicts of Jesus assemblies, some of which Paul established, others that he joined, and at least one that he did not know personally.

But six of the thirteen letters have enough differences in style, vocabulary, and content from the undisputed letters to warrant the question: Did Paul write these? The disputed letters are divided into the Deutero-Pauline letters—Colossians, Ephesians, and 2 Thessalonians—and the pastoral letters—1 and 2 Timothy, and Titus. If Paul did not write these letters, who did and why? Why write under his name?

Over the course of the nineteenth and twentieth centuries, with the skills and perspective of critical biblical scholarship, Paul scholars arrived at a consensus—with slightly more agreement for 2 Thessalonians than for Colossians, for example—that these six letters were written toward the end of the first century or even at the beginning of the second century. Paul died around 62 or 64 C.E. Demurral from this judgment comes largely, though not exclusively, from more conservative scholars for whom Paul's authority for the letters is paramount.

The question of who wrote the disputed letters is still an open one. Some describe the anonymous writers as a "Pauline school" or disciples of Paul. Either designation assumes a certain kind of relation to Paul. But it is perhaps more important to ask what they were doing and why they drew on Paul's authority. Leaving aside the who question, then, here I pursue the why question.

DIFFERENCE

Critical judgment about authorship requires technical skills and scholarly methods, especially of textual criticism. But differences in the perspective of a text, as the Galatians and 1 Corinthians example showed above, can be seen by even the casual reader. I will take three brief examples of the authentic and inauthentic letters on three important topics: ministry, women, and slavery.

1. Ministry

Now concerning spiritual gifts, brothers and sisters. . . . To each is given the manifestation of the Spirit for the common good. . . . For in the one Spirit we were all baptized into one body. . . . Now you are the body of Christ and individually members of it. And God has appointed in the *ekklēsia* first apostles, second prophets, third

The saying is sure: whoever aspires to the office of bishop desires a noble task. Now a bishop must be above reproach, married only once. . . . He must manage his own household well. . . . Deacons likewise must be serious. . . . Let deacons be married only once, and let them manage their children and households well.

teachers; then deeds of power, then gifts of healing, forms of assistance, forms of leadership, various kinds of tongues.

2. Women

As many of you as were baptized into Christ have clothed yourselves with Christ. There is no longer Jew or Greek, there is no longer slave or free, there is no longer male and female; for all of you are one in Christ Jesus.

I permit no woman to teach or to have authority over a man; she is to keep silent. For Adam was formed first, then Eve; and Adam was not deceived, but the woman was deceived and became a transgressor. Yet she will be saved through childbearing, provided they continue in faith and love and holiness, with modesty.

3. Slavery

Perhaps this is the reason Onesimus was separated from you for awhile, so that you might have him back forever, no longer

Let all who are under the yoke of slavery regard their masters as worthy of honor. . . . Those who have believing

as a slave but more
than a slave, a beloved
brother—especially to
me but how much
more to you, both in
the flesh and in the
Lord. . . . Welcome
him as you would
welcome me.

masters . . . must serve
them all the more.

Would the same person write both the statements on the left and right? Would the same person proclaim equality to one audience and demand subjugation from another? Would one person argue such radically different positions? Do these positions point to different times or situations in the life of one author, or do they point to alternative views of two authors? These texts are not neutral. They reflect persons and interests of masters, slaves, husbands, wives. The social reality they create is different. Persons are named as equals in one, as nonpersons in another. Single words carry radically different kinds of status: master, slave. Androcentric interests shape theological concepts: women's salvation is dependent on childbearing.

Determination of authorship comes from comparing the disputed and undisputed texts and being attentive to each and every difference. Paul and the anonymous authors share the language of their culture, but they each make it their own—favoring some words, avoiding others, for example, or tending to construct their sentences in certain ways and never others. Each has a background horizon, a worldview that shapes their concerns. Even their grammatical mistakes constitute a kind of signature of their own. Comparing texts will turn up these differences.

The clues may appear inconsequential. In referring to creation, for example, Colossians cites "all things in heaven and on earth, things visible and invisible" (1:16). The contrast here between visible and invisible is not an expression found in the undisputed letters. So, too, the Colossian expression "endure everything with patience" (1:11) is not one common to Paul.

A more significant clue is the absence of a characteristic theme of Paul's in a disputed text. Colossians lacks the eschatological urgency that permeated Paul's whole way of thinking. His initial mystical experience was filled with eschatological symbolism and meaning. His letters are full of references to the coming day of wrath. If Paul is the writer of Colossians, it is harder to explain the absence of this theme in this letter than to introduce the possibility of a second author.

Another important theme in the authentic letters is the Holy Spirit. The Spirit is the power that transforms the pagan behavior of Gentiles and heads them toward a life of holiness. It provides the gifts for charismatic leadership and fills the needs of the assembly with other gifts. The list of sins in Colossians 3:5–17 sounds very much like Paul's lists but without the Spirit empowering the reorientation of Gentile life toward the good. The Spirit is especially significant for Paul because the reception of the Spirit is, in his judgment, the primary validation of his position that observance of the law is not a requirement for Gentile inclusion in God's salvation. Would Paul write a letter without invoking the Spirit?

Yet with the notable absence of eschatological urgency
and the Spirit, Colossians is also very much like the genuine letters of Paul. It was, after all, mistaken for Paul's own
for centuries. Some sentences are almost verbatim. In an
appeal for personal renewal, for example, the Colossians
author writes:

> There is no longer Greek and Jew, circumcised and uncircum-
> cised, barbarian, Scythian, slave and free; but Christ is all and
> in all! (3:11)

We have already seen a close parallel to this text in
Galatians. Paul integrates what is thought to be a fragment from the baptismal ceremony that women and men
undergo as an initiation ritual into the eschatological
assembly.[1] It is woven into Paul's argument that all are
children of God through faith (3:26):

> There is no longer Jew or Greek, there is no longer slave or
> free, there is no longer male and female; for all of you are one
> in Christ Jesus. (3:28)

The contrasts are forms of privilege. The first contrast
is not political but religious or ethnic: the covenant insider
versus the covenant outsider. The second is class: the privilege of the slave owner versus human property. The third is
gender: the privilege of male versus female. This third relation is missing in Colossians.

In the Pauline assemblies membership is inclusive.
Women and men are members of the assembly by the same
entrance rite. Their membership is on an equal basis. The
expression "no longer male or female" does not pretend

that the biological distinctness of male and female has disappeared but that male nature does not now have a normative value that female nature lacks by virtue of being not-male. Women are persons, not property defined by their reproductive capacity.

Gender privilege—male dominance—is for Paul on the side of a sinful world, as is the case for the other two forms of privilege. They are part of the dynamics of a fallen world. Redemption restores the goodness of creation. The distorted relations between religions, between masters and slaves, and between women and men can be redeemed, as they are by Christ's life, death, and resurrection. An eschatological and egalitarian assembly embodies this redemptive restoration.

There could be many reasons why Colossians does not have the third contrast of the baptismal fragment. Perhaps the author knew this saying from another source that reflected Galatians 3:28. But it may be that the writer does not consider gender domination to be a distortion of creation.

Instead of the expressions of equality found in the undisputed letters, Colossians reinforced the reigning cultural paradigm of familial and other social relationships and interactions. It may have the most quoted of any New Testament passages: "Wives, be subject to your husbands. . . . Slaves obey your earthly masters" (3:18, 22). These passages have been the biblical foundation for women's subordination and the social institution of slavery. They are drawn from a cultural "household code" that prescribes proper relations within the patriarchal family.

In the hierarchical structure of the patriarchal household, the subordinate members owe obedience to the male head of the family. Their duty is not voluntary. They are, in fact, the property of the head male. The highly stratified world of the empire was modeled on the patriarchal household. Obedience to authority is the central value in a domination system.

For the Colossians author, the relations and structure of the patriarchal household do not belong to the evil age from which Christ's death has set human beings free (Gal 1:4) but remain normative for the present and future. Further, they are not just relevant for the social world of family and empire but for the assembly as well. The code inserted by the Colossians author instructs subordinates in the household—wives, children, slaves—with brief remarks to husbands, fathers, and masters:

> Wives, be subject to your husbands, as is fitting in the Lord. Husbands, love your wives and never treat them harshly. Children, obey your parents in everything, for this is your acceptable duty in the Lord. Fathers, do not provoke your children, or they may lose heart. Slaves, obey your earthly masters in everything, not only while being watched and in order to please them, but wholeheartedly, fearing the Lord. Whatever your task, put yourselves into it, as done for the Lord and not for your masters, since you know that from the Lord you will receive the inheritance as your reward; you serve the Lord Christ. For the wrongdoer will be paid back for whatever wrong has been done, and there is no partiality. Masters, treat your slaves justly and fairly, for you know that you also have a Master in heaven. (Col 3:18–4:1)

The letter to the Ephesians also cites a household code. Whether Ephesians was actually a letter is a question I will bracket here. It is enough that it functioned as a letter. It has an elaborate section directed to the husband that integrates Paul's body theology—the assembly is the body of Christ and members are part of the body. While the extensive instructions to the husband seem to even out the code for husband and wife, in fact, they do not. The husband is told to love his wife, but she is to be subject to him in everything as the assembly is to the cosmic Christ. He is head of the wife. In effect, then, Christian values in Ephesians have not transformed the status of wife as property but Christianized the patriarchal code by making masters equivalent to Christ. The Ephesians code is longer than the one in Colossians. I quote it in full:[2]

> Wives, be subject to your husbands as you are to the Lord. For the husband is the head of the wife just as Christ is the head of the church, the body of which he is the Savior. Just as the church is subject to Christ, so also wives ought to be, in everything, to their husbands.
>
> Husbands, love your wives, just as Christ loved the church and gave himself up for her, in order to make her holy by cleansing her with the washing of water by the word, so as to present the church to himself in splendor, without a spot or wrinkle or anything of the kind—yes, so that she may be holy and without blemish. In the same way, husbands should love their wives as they do their own bodies. He who loves his wife loves himself. For no one ever hates his own body, but he nourishes and tenderly cares for it, just as Christ does for the church, because we are members of his body. For this reason a man will leave his father and mother and be joined

to his wife, and the two will become one flesh. This is a great mystery, and I am applying it to Christ and the church. Each of you, however, should love his wife as himself, and a wife should respect her husband.

Children, obey your parents in the Lord, for this is right. "Honor your father and mother"—this is the first commandment with a promise: "so that it may be well with you and you may live long on the earth."

And, fathers, do not provoke your children to anger, but bring them up in the discipline and instruction of the Lord.

Slaves, obey your earthly masters with fear and trembling, in singleness of heart, as you obey Christ: not only while being watched, and in order to please them, but as slaves of Christ, doing the will of God from the heart. Render the service with enthusiasm, as to the Lord and not to men and women, knowing whatever good we do, we will receive the same again from the Lord, whether we are slaves or free. And, masters, do the same to them. Stop threatening them, for you know that both of you have the same Master in heaven, and with him there is no partiality. (Eph 5:22–6:9)

A third New Testament letter, attributed to Jesus' disciple Peter but also likely written by an anonymous writer near the end of the century, also integrates a household code (2:18–3:7). Wives again are instructed to accept the authority of husbands (3:1); husbands are to honor the woman as the weaker sex (3:7); and slaves are to accept the authority of their masters, even those who are harsh (2:18). Obedience and submission are overriding values of this author. The instructions for the assembly follow:

For the Lord's sake accept the authority of every human institution, whether the emperor as supreme, or of the governors, as

sent by him to punish those who do wrong and to praise those
who do right. . . . Honor the emperor. (2:13–14, 17)

With the household the model for the assembly, relations among persons as well as the structure of the assembly will be the same as the household. The fundamental
distortion highlighted in Galatians 3:28 as overcome by
Christ's redemption is reappropriated here as normative.
The assembly divides into separate and unequal spheres.
Subordinate members owe obedience and submission to
those who rule. The messiness of charismatic governance is
replaced by order and office filled by appropriate persons.

The women and men Paul converted created a social
reality from their transformed values. Responding to
the message of redemption transformed their relations.
People separated by class, gender, and ethnic or religious
status in the patriarchal world were united by a radical ethic of equality in the assembly. Paul's expression,
"being in Christ," had a present, social meaning signaled
for Gentiles by Galatians 3:28.

By the end of the century, however, Paul's ethic of
equality was meeting with active resistance. Cynthia Briggs
Kittredge writes that the problem became that "Paul's earlier letters are read through the lens of the later letters,
which sharply curtail women's leadership and limit the role
of women to accepting their subordinate position in the
Greco-Roman patriarchal household."[3] Elisabeth Schüssler
Fiorenza describes the Deutero-Pauline letters "as a struggle between the egalitarian impulses of early Christianity
and those forces that would organize the church along the
lines of the traditional patriarchal household."[4]

This time, however, the challenge to Paul did not come from fellow Jesus evangelists coming into one of his assemblies to oppose his gospel directly, but from other writers appropriating his voice for views of their own. These examples are from 1 Timothy:

- In Paul's name, they cite household codes to designate normative structures for the assembly; domination is embraced as God's will, not rejected as sinful.
- In Paul's name, they instruct men to pray properly and women to dress properly: "I desire, then, that in every place men should pray . . . women should dress themselves modestly and decently in suitable clothing" (2:8–9).
- In Paul's name, they direct women to behave as the patriarchal world expects: "Let a woman learn in silence with full submission" (2:11).
- In Paul's name, they insist on separate and unequal gender spheres in the assembly: "I permit no woman to teach or have authority over a man; she is to keep silent" (2:12).
- In Paul's name, they ground woman's subordination in Genesis 2: "For Adam was formed first, then Eve: and Adam was not deceived, but the woman was deceived and became a transgressor" (2:13–14).
- In Paul's name, they make woman's salvation dependent on acquiescence to her reproductive role in creation: "Yet she will be saved through childbearing, provided they continue in faith and love and holiness, with modesty" (2:15).

- In Paul's name, they name the assembly the household of God (3:15).

The Deutero-Pauline and pastoral authors make obedience to those who rule a religious obligation. They maintain the status quo by making disobedience sin. The voice who commands obedience in the text is that of the slave owner. The slave owner identifies himself with Christ, grounding his rule in the cosmic headship of Christ.

Paul has one passage about headship in 1 Corinthians 11:3–16. He, too, refers implicitly to Genesis 2–3 as the grounds for gender hierarchy, but he balances this with the note that man comes through woman. His appeal to headship is in the context of an elaborate argument about hairstyles and prophecy and what is appropriate to men and to women. Is it proper for a woman to pray to God with her head unveiled? The issue is praying with or without a head covering and hairstyles, not praying itself. It is gender conventions that Paul seeks here, not the exclusion of women from participating in the assembly.

In considering the treatment of women by the rabbis in the Mishnah, a postbiblical interpretation of the Torah, Ross Kraemer notes that "the intensification of prescriptions against women is often a response to the increased autonomy and authority of women."[5] To see the integration of the household codes in this light is instructive. We have suggested in our discussion of the Galatian conflict that those who opposed Paul's gospel may have been scandalized not only by the unrestricted social interaction between Jew and Gentile but also by the unrestricted social interaction between women and men, too. Whether these authors were so scandalized is an open question, but it is nonetheless virtually impossible to avoid the conclusion that they did not want men and women to be equal members of the assembly.

We now know in retrospect that the inclusive charismatic governance characteristic of the Pauline assemblies did not last long after Paul's own life and ministry. The active participation of women in the early church has been erased from the historical record. The tendency of androcentric texts to make women invisible occurs even as early as the Gospel of Mark, dated around 70 C.E. by most. Mark does not mention women disciples until Mark 15:40, just prior to the story of the women disciples discovering the empty tomb and receiving the message that Jesus had been raised from the dead. As Karen Jo Torjesen writes of the first four centuries, women were engaged in various roles for some time:

> Despite the androcentric retelling of women's stories, treatises from this first formative period reveal that women were apostles, prophets, and teachers; that they exercised a diversity of ministries including baptizing, disciplining, and presiding over the Eucharist; and that they held the full range of church offices—bishop, presbyter, widow, deacon, and virgin.[6]

But the Deutero-Pauline letters show that pressure was on from the first century to realign the assembly with patriarchal culture and to rein in women from independent involvement in the movement. Bonnie Bowman Thurston writes, "Restrictions placed on women reflect the writer's discomfort with their influence and power.

Subordination to male authority is made a test of appropriate Christian behavior."[7]

The Deutero-Pauline and pastoral authors are not describing women in their communities but rather are prescribing—as Kraemer says of the rabbis in the Mishnah—what they want women to be and to do. If women were silent and submissive in their assemblies, they would not have to be instructed to be so. The authors are attempting to change an existing situation. Bonnie Thurston makes this point: "That so much space is devoted to behavior appropriate to women shows that women were, in fact, prominent in Christian communities."[8] Why would the writer do so? Thurston writes, "The Pastoral writer limits their activity precisely because it was important and influential."[9]

The liberation of women from male rule and the granting of social and political rights were modern secular achievements. Christian communities have followed suit—more or less—by allowing women more equal participation and leadership with men. Not all have been in favor of peeling away the authority of Paul from the Deutero-Pauline letters. If the headship of the male in marriage is desired, for example, then the Deutero-Pauline letters are more important than the authentic letters. Male headship can be supported by a text or two in the authentic letters, but overall there is more authority for equality there than for domination.

PRESERVATION OR SUBVERSION

What were these writers doing when they took Paul's name for letters of their own? Among scholars one finds two basic answers. One answer is that the Deutero-Pauline authors were engaged in the preservation, interpretation, or extension of Paul's convictions. This position assumes that they value Paul's views and want to influence their own situation with them. The second answer is subversion. This position argues that the authors wanted to change Paul and they proceed to do so under his own name. One scholar argues the first position:

> I also assume that the six other letters attributed to Paul are Deutero-Pauline written at a later time and from a later perspective. I believe, however, that they reflect genuinely Pauline ideas, consistent with or developing Paul's thought. Some scholars posit the existence of a "Pauline school" that could have been responsible for preserving and fostering Paul's letters. Some colleagues or disciples of Paul may have considered it their duty to preserve and evolve Paul's teachings.[10]

I would argue exactly the opposite case. The redemptive equality that characterizes the Pauline communities cannot be found in the perspective of the Deutero-Pauline letters. The participation and leadership of women reflected, for example, in Romans 16, is countered by the reappropriation of patriarchal norms and structures that silence and cause the submission of women. The Deutero-Pauline authors used Paul's voice to communicate their opposition to the egalitarianism of the Jesus assemblies. The inauthentic letters provided the biblical foundation for the subordination of women and the social institution of slavery up to modern times.[11] The authentic letters could not have provided such a justification.

The literary judgment that distinguished Paul's own letters from the ones written in his name did much more than settle a practical question of authorship. It liberated Paul from being the spokesperson for patriarchy and all it represents—among other things, hierarchy, relations of domination and subordination, and separate and unequal gender spheres. The values in the authentic and inauthentic letters are starkly different from one another. What the inauthentic letters communicate is that one can be Christian and still consider other human beings property—women (as a male), and slaves (as an owner). This is absolutely contradictory to Paul's ethic of "living in the Spirit" (Gal 5:16) and to his appeal to love as the greatest of gifts (1 Cor 12). Sinfulness is the absence of love, as Bernard Lonergan defines sin here: "Sinfulness is distinct from moral evil; it is the privation of total loving; it is a radical dimension of lovelessness."[12] The Deutero-Pauline letters make such sin appear sacred.

SLAVERY

Among the several biblical words for sin, *hamartia*, "missing the mark," is the most common. What mark does sin miss? In the broadest sense, sin misses the mark of the human good.

Slavery is the most radical example of missing the good of others. It goes beyond the denial of their rights and opportunities to the denial of their very humanity. Aristotle called a slave a human tool. Since the earliest human history, the elite of many cultures have generated wealth for themselves from the exploitation of others. Class stratification divides the haves and the have-nots into separate spheres where the haves take the full resources of the social order for themselves, leaving the have-nots without fulfillment of even their most basic needs.

Historians have often accounted for slavery in the ancient world as something that was so much part of the cultural fabric of people's lives that they did not even see it as evil.

But the work of Orlando Patterson brought into clearer focus that incredible violence is required to sustain slavery.[13] The evil of slavery is revealed by what it takes to keep slaves captive. Richard Horsley points to the pervading sense of insecurity among elites in the Roman empire who depended on slaves for their positions of wealth and power.[14] Ancient texts speak of masters dying violently at the hands of their slaves, the danger of owning slaves, and the potential for slave revolt. Slaves resisted in whatever way they could. Those in the slaveholding class agreed that it was necessary to create fear among their slaves. Tactics of dehumanization and degradation were deliberate: slave markets in which slaves were exhibited naked, repeated selling of slaves, restraint by chains, branding and tattooing, beating, torture, and sexual exploitation.

Slavery is a coercive system. No one would choose to be a slave if things could be otherwise. This is the reason for the inordinate amount of violence inflicted on slaves. We cannot reasonably imagine that slavery was different for Christian slave owners than for others in their culture. Slave owners used various tactics of violence to keep slaves from fleeing or revolting. Slaves were bodies. They could be worked to death in fields or mines, given domestic duties of little consequence, and sexually exploited at their master's will. As Jennifer Glancy emphasizes, a slave could not say no. Slave bodies were available to the master for two primary purposes, first for the purpose of the master's sexual gratification, and second for providing enslaved offspring for the future.[15]

While it may be true that people took slavery for granted, that may say more about historians' sense that the interests that create slavery are too entrenched in human beings to be eradicated, not that the ancients were unaware of its moral reprehensibility. Slaves themselves were certainly aware of the evil done to them. Moreover, slaveholders were not blind to the economic benefits of free labor.[16] It is a safe assumption that the massive building projects that glorified the regimes of many ancient kings would not have been undertaken if paid labor had been their only option.

Emancipatory impulses cast further suspicion on the view that the ancients could not see the injustice of slavery. Jesus' vision of God's *basileia* is of a domination-free order. Paul integrates a baptismal fragment into his letter to the Galatians that clearly rejects class domination (3:28). Paul's assertion that slave and free are "no longer" puts slavery in the "present evil age" (1:4), thus on the side of sinful reality. It contrasts inequality and equality as categories of sin and redemption. What replaces class stratification is an inclusive community that restores the original equality of human beings symbolized in the first Genesis creation story.

In addition to emancipatory impulses, the justifications of slavery themselves are evidence of the desire to mask its moral evil and to shift the blame from the oppressor to oppressed. The economic self-interest of the slaveholder is never mentioned. Slavery is explained by way of something in its victims—their deficiency in nature, their birth, or their punishment for sin. Aristotle argued that from the "hour of their birth some are marked out for subjection."[17] In the American South, slaveholders promoted an image of slaves as children, graciously made members of the plantation family by the plantation owner who cared for "his people."[18] Until the end of World War II, the preeminent historian of slavery in the United States was Ulrich Phillips. He portrayed blacks as childlike and inferior to whites. His picture of the plantation was idyllic—blacks were better off influenced by Christianity and civilization than back in Africa. Phillips defended both the slave economy and slaveholders.[19]

As a social institution, religion can promote or offset the interests of the powerful in the public domain. In Walter Brueggemann's terms, a religion of legitimation furthers an oppressive politics and exploitative economics.[20] Religion promotes the economic interests of the elite when theologians describe slavery as part of the order of creation or when it is denied that slaves are human beings in possession of the image of God, or even in possession of a human soul. Scriptures can reinforce the status quo. The Deutero-Pauline slavery texts were virtually the whole of Scripture for white preachers in the American South who were used by plantation owners to give divine sanction to a slave economy.

The fact that we can find in Scripture both oppressive and liberating texts points to a fundamental ambiguity in Scripture itself. The ambiguity has its source in the fact that meaning can be distorted. Evil can be rationalized

as good. Theological concepts such as sin can be shaped
to serve the ends of the powerful who control religious
symbols. An ideological concept of sin reinforces obedience to those who rule. It portrays their privilege as
divinely willed. Ideological texts divide social reality into
separate and unequal spheres. They sanctify oppressive and
exploitative social systems as ordained by God. Injustice is
portrayed as necessary to this world. Hints that it will be
rectified in the next world do not necessarily exonerate
those responsible for the injustice.

The influence of the Deutero-Pauline and pastoral
authors in the history of slavery is unparalleled. They gave
the scriptural foundation for the Christian justification of
slavery. God wills the service of slaves to Christian masters.
The texts Christianize the relation between master and
slave. These four texts provided Christian theologians with
the revelatory basis for the social institution of slavery.

Paul's First Letter to Timothy

The writer of 1 Timothy makes honoring slave masters
equivalent to honoring God. The fact that disrespect of
believing masters must be explicitly prohibited suggests tensions between converted slaveholders and converted slaves
in this Jesus assembly:

> Let all who are under the yoke of slavery regard their masters
> as worthy of all honor, so that the name of God and the teach-
> ing may not be blasphemed. Those who have believing masters
> must not be disrespectful to them on the ground that they are
> members of the church; rather they must serve them all the

more, since those who benefit by their service are believers and
beloved. (6:1–2)

Paul's Letter to the Colossians

The author of Colossians identifies slave owners with
Christ. Serving one's master is serving Christ. Or to reverse
the image, refusal of the master is refusal of Christ. The
conclusion need not be stated: disobedience of Christ is sin.
The author's instruction for Christian slave owners to treat
their slaves "justly and fairly" ignores the fact that slavery is
itself the most extreme injustice that a human being could
endure.

> Slaves, obey your earthly masters in everything, not only while
> being watched and in order to please them, but wholeheart-
> edly, fearing the Lord. Whatever your task, put yourselves into
> it, as done for the Lord and not for your masters, since you
> know that from the Lord you will receive the inheritance as
> your reward; you serve the Lord Christ. For the wrongdoer will
> be paid back for whatever wrong has been done, and there is
> no partiality. Masters, treat your slaves justly and fairly, for you
> know that you also have a Master in heaven. (3:22–4:1)

Paul's Letter to the Ephesians

The author of Ephesians depicts the work of slaves
as God's will, grounding their duty not simply in their
labor but in their feelings and desires. The slave master is
identified with Christ: obeying one is obeying the other.
Again, what is unspoken but understood is that disobeying
Christ—the master—is sin. The instruction to masters to

stop threatening their slaves suggests the reality of violence that accompanies the slave–master relationship, no less in Christian slaveholding than in non-Christian:

> Slaves, obey your earthly masters with fear and trembling, in singleness of heart, as you obey Christ: not only while being watched, and in order to please them, but as slaves of Christ, doing the will of God from the heart. Render the service with enthusiasm, as to the Lord and not to men and women, knowing whatever good we do, we will receive the same again from the Lord, whether we are slaves or free. And, masters, do the same to them. Stop threatening them, for you know that both of you have the same Master in heaven, and with him there is no partiality. (3:22–6:9)

The First Letter of Peter

In one of the few household texts outside the Pauline corpus, 1 Peter sanctifies the suffering of the slave, linking it with the suffering of Christ, claiming even the model of Christ's suffering for slavery. It acknowledges the harshness—violence—endured by the slave but requires that this, too, be accepted. God's approval is asserted for the suffering:

> Slaves, accept the authority of your masters with all deference, not only those who are kind and gentle but also those who are harsh. For it is a credit to you if, being aware of God, you endure pain while suffering unjustly. If you endure when you are beaten for doing wrong, what credit is that? But if you endure when you do right and suffer for it, you have God's approval. For to this you have been called, because Christ also

suffered for you, leaving you an example, so that you should follow in his steps. (2:18–21)

The Deutero-Pauline and pastoral texts sanctified enslaved existence as God's will. They Christianized the oppressive relation of master to slave by identifying the Christian slave owner with Christ, on the one hand, and, on the other, glorifying the suffering of the slave by identifying it with Christ's suffering.

The slavery texts are oddly dispassionate. No nod of sympathy is extended to the slave, no acknowledgment of the experiential realities known by everyone—the violence inflicted by masters to keep slaves from escape, the extreme physical, sexual, and mental suffering experienced by slaves, the despair incurred in being torn from families and homes. No acknowledgment is made of the wealth that flowed to the slave owners by virtue of the exploited labor of slaves. The reader tends to adopt this dispassionate tone and ignore the implications of what is being said.

Augustine, Bishop of Hippo, assumed the Deutero-Pauline scripture as his foundation when in the fifth century he proposed—the first in the Christian tradition to do so—that slavery is divinely ordained of God and that perpetual bondage had apostolic sanction.[21] In contrast to Aristotle, who argued that slavery was natural, Augustine argued that slavery was unnatural. It did not come with creation but rather with the fall. Because original sin is permanent, so too is the institution of slavery.

The medieval theologian Thomas Aquinas qualified Aristotle's idea that some human beings are by nature slaves. Aristotle's reason for arguing a theory of "natural slavery" had to do with justice.[22] If slavery were not natural to some, the relation between master and slave would rest on force alone, which would be unjust. But if slavery is natural, then the issue is how to rule slaves and that is a matter of justice.

Thomas was personally appalled by slavery, but because it was an "unbroken tradition" in the church and in the civil order, he accepted it. He defended holding slaves as private property.[23] While documents point to criticisms of slavery throughout the tradition, the social institution itself was accepted as part of the created order. Regulations of Christian ownership of slaves do appear in church councils and papal documents such as these:

- Council of Agde, 506: regulations, slaves of the church, for example, protection of a manumitted slave by the church
- Pope Gregory III, 731: prohibition on Christian sale of slaves to pagans for sacrificial rites
- Council of Worms, 876: prohibition against Christians killing their slaves

In the eighteenth century, Brazilian Bishop Azenedo Coutinho—himself from a slaveholding family—defended the legitimacy of the Atlantic slave trade in his book, *Analysis of the Justice of the Slave Trade on the Mina Coast* (1798). Antislavery books were put on the Vatican's Index of Forbidden Books.

In nineteenth-century America, Catholic bishops such as Bishop John England and Archbishop John Hughes resisted any criticisms of American slavery coming from the

Vatican. They opposed abolition. The bishops saw slavery as a political issue, not a moral one. Their failure to condemn slavery was not unrelated to the fact that both Protestant and Catholic clergy owned slaves. This was the chief factor in their justification of slavery as a social institution. A classic defense of slavery was written by George Armstrong, *The Christian Doctrine of Slavery*, in 1857.

Southern ministers in the United States were among the strongest defenders of slavery in the eighteenth and nineteenth centuries, calling it a "divine institution." Some owned sizable plantations and large numbers of slaves.[24] Much slave labor was put to the service of cotton, the chief export of the United States. Because it required cheap labor to make it profitable, the southern colonies were committed to a slave economy. "In 1792," James Poling writes, "the nation raised 6,000 bales of cotton; by 1810, 178,000." The difference in production and profit was attributable to free labor. Slave labor created wealth for both the North and South.

Cotton Mather, an influential Puritan minister, supported slavery and was himself a slaveholder. He was an active proponent of converting slaves. He advised Christian slave owners that Christianized slaves would be more efficient and that Scripture had no law forbidding servitude. The slave owners were duty bound, Mather said, to teach their slaves "that it is God who has caused them to be Servants, and that they serve Jesus Christ, while they are at Work for their Masters."[25] The economic interests of slave owners remained unacknowledged. The cause for slavery was to be found in the slave. Mather argued that Negroes were enslaved because they had sinned against God.

The Catholic Church accepted slavery until 1891 and its official rejection in Pope Leo XIII's *Rerum Novarium*. Britain outlawed slavery in 1830. The United States did so in 1863. Theologically, the church's rejection of slavery required a reversal in the way in which the Pauline texts were interpreted. If they were not a direct revelation of God's will, how were they to be understood? This raised the difficult issue of the relation between God and the text—are there human interests that the text reflects that are at odds with what God would want?

Today, still, some fundamentalist "reconstructionist Christians" advocate the legitimacy of slavery. But most Christian traditions have apologized in some way for their past views on slavery or segregation. One of the last to do so was the Southern Baptist Convention, which in 1995 passed a resolution that slavery was sinful and asked forgiveness from blacks for its historic role in defending segregation.[26] This was a reversal of its previous position that God had ordained the separation of races and that to tamper with this separation was to go against God's will.

QUESTIONS FOR
REFLECTION AND DISCUSSION

1. Do the disputed letters make the matter of a normative canon problematic? How? How have the disputed letters been a larger problem for Paul than his opponents from Jerusalem?
2. Much has been made of the tradition of the household codes quoted from Colossians and Ephesians.

Why are these texts so significant? How have they been used?

3. Preservation or subversion: which would you choose for the authors of the letters attributed to Paul? What were they doing?

4. Southern slave owners in the United States were active proponents of the disputed letters. With them as a foundation, what could they say about slavery? If you were a Christian at that time who believed Scripture was revelatory but were against slavery (and did not know the letters were disputed), what could you say in response to the slave owner? Write a one-page response.

The *Adversus Judaeos* Tradition

The historical Paul shifted loyalties from one Jewish party to another. Identifying early on with the Pharisees, he made a radical change from opposing the messianic Jews to being one of them, raising no little suspicion on the part of some (Gal 1:13). He was steeped in the apocalyptic images and ideas of the end time that they announced. Eschatological hopes and expectations crossed the boundaries of Jewish groups. As a Pharisee and as a Jesus follower Paul hoped for a future day when God would overcome conditions that distort creation. God's agent would come in judgment to punish evildoers and vindicate the righteous. The event of resurrection would signal the beginning of the end time.

Paul did not come to faith in Christ through hearing the preaching of disciples such as James and Peter. His turnabout was due to an intensely personal mystical experience in which God revealed the risen Christ to him (Gal 15). Like the Hebrew prophets before him, Paul was called by God to do something. His commission was to extend God's offer of salvation to non-Jews. Thus his self-designation "apostle to the Gentiles."

To Paul and other Jews in the first century, the first condition for salvation was belonging to the covenant community of Israel. As we indicated earlier, Paul's very nuanced idea of what was expected of Gentiles for their inclusion in Israel was based on his understanding of the death and resurrection of Jesus. In this chapter we explore the most influential, if woefully mistaken, tradition of interpreting Paul—and its tragic consequences.

OUTSIDERS BROUGHT IN

As we have seen, Paul drew specific meaning for Gentiles from Jesus' death. He presumed the sacrificial nature of Christ's death, an interpretation formulated by Jesus followers before him. The Gentiles were in a position to accept God's offer of salvation because Christ had paid their debt for sin.

Like the crucified one, Gentiles are named by the law as outsiders. God's validation of Jesus in raising him from the dead signaled God's openness to other outsiders. If this is so, the law—which mandates its own observance—must no longer be normative. The inclusion of Gentiles is not dependent, as the law would have it, on their becoming Jews. Now, Paul argued, the condition for Gentile membership, and thus for salvation, is faith in Christ. The conclusion to all this—that Gentiles as Gentiles are now included in Israel's covenant—is expressed in the compact phrase, the "truth of the gospel" (Gal 2:14).[1]

Paul's insistence that Gentiles did not have to appropriate a Jewish lifestyle contradicted the prevalent positions of the time. Jews held different opinions about Gentile converts, but underlying the range of differences was the dominant view that if Gentiles wanted to share in the biblical promises given to Israel, they had to become Jews to do so. Men underwent the ritual of circumcision, taking on the sign of membership mandated by God to Abraham (Gen 17:10). The initiation ritual for women was baptism. Once initiated with circumcision and baptism, they were Jewish men and women under the obligation to observe the law as native-born Jews were so obligated.

INTERPRETATION

From the earliest time in the Christian tradition, Paul's letters were a source of inspiration. They were mined by Christian theologians for their insights on the purpose and meaning of Christ's life, death, and resurrection as well as the purpose and meaning of the believer's life and future. Who are we? What is our purpose? What will happen next? These questions constitute an underlying current generating theological reflection in the first centuries of the church. But, in retrospect, there were as many misunderstandings of Paul that contributed to a distorted interpretation of what he was saying. Several misunderstandings of particular import are these:

- *Conversion.* The experience of conversion has been understood as Paul's reason for changing from an inferior religion to a superior one. In embracing Christianity, he rejected all of Judaism.
- *Conflict.* Corresponding to the idea of superior and inferior religions, "faith in Christ" and "works of the law" were thought to reflect superior and inferior religions, with faith the superior, too.
- *Works of the law.* Christian interpreters presumed that by "works" Paul meant "doing things to merit one's own salvation." This was the basis for the judgment that Judaism was a religion of "works righteousness." They took his conversion as a rejection of Judaism, the law, and works righteousness.
- *Rejection of Israel.* Christians throughout the tradition have denounced the Jews for killing Jesus. They read Paul's polemical language about the Jews as a confirmation that God's covenant with the Jews had ended. They overlooked indications to the contrary, such as Paul's remarks in Romans that "all Israel will be saved" (11:26) and that "the gifts and the calling of God are irrevocable" (11:29). Ignored, too, was the question he raised and answered: "I ask, then, has God rejected his people? By no means!" (11:1). How the election of Israel and salvation by Christ fit together is a theological problem for Paul, but he

does not resolve it by ending the covenant relation between Israel and God.

SHIFTING BLAME

Paul does not name names, but there are still indications on his part that Jesus' death was due to imperial powers. It is suggested in remarks like this: "None of the rulers of this age understood this, for if they had, they would not have crucified the Lord of glory" (1 Cor 2:8). Veiled allusions set the redemptive role of Christ against the empire: "Grace to you and peace from God the Father and the Lord Jesus Christ, who gave himself for our sins to set us free from the present evil age" (Gal 1:3).

Other passages challenge the empire with visions of its destruction: "Then comes the end, when he hands over the kingdom to God the Father, after he has destroyed every ruler and every authority and power" (1 Cor 15:24).

But within decades of Jesus' crucifixion at the hands of Rome, the historical memory among Jesus followers began to change. By the end of the century, the original Jewish messianic movement was largely constituted by Gentiles. The injustice of the Romans disappeared, replaced by the evil done to Jesus by the Jews. Matthew creates: "Then the people as a whole answered, His blood be on us and our children!" (Matt 27:25–26). Later Christians read this simply as history, thinking that it reflected what happened. The idea that the author could construct scenes in which the reader sees clearly who is to blame—and that this was in fact constructed to do exactly this—would be a modern discovery.

In blaming the Jews for Jesus' death, the Gospel writers had to deal with the fact that crucifixion was a death inflicted on persons suspected of subversive actions. It was only Roman imperial authorities who could carry out this favored method of execution. Even Herod the Great, a Jewish king allowed to rule under the Romans, was not allowed to put someone to death by crucifixion. But in the Gospels, it is the chief priests who arrest Jesus. Pilate is only involved because the chief priests bring Jesus to him to crucify, saying, "We are not permitted to put anyone to death" (John 18:18–31).

Written in the second half of the first century, perhaps even in the second century, Christian writings replaced Romans with Jews in the story of Jesus' death. In the Gospel of Luke the "chief priests and scribes were looking for a way to put Jesus to death" (Luke 22:2). It is "the chief priests, the officers of the temple police, and the elders" who come to arrest Jesus (22:52). The Romans were given the role of simply carrying out what the Jews wanted done. In the Gospel of John, Pilate says to Jesus, "Your own nation and chief priests have handed you over to me" (18:35). Pilate even allows a mob to choose whom to release from prison. He asks the crowd gathered outside if they want a bandit released or Jesus: "They shouted in reply, 'Not this man, but Barabbas!'" (18:40). In the Gospel of Mark, Barabbas is described as "in prison with the rebels who had committed murder during the insurrection" (15:7). For Pilate to release an insurrectionist would have been highly out of character, to say the least.

Relieved of the villainous murder of Jesus, the Romans had more positive roles in the Gospels. In the Gospel of

Mark, for instance, it is a centurion—a Gentile Roman soldier—who proclaims Jesus to be God's Son at the crucifixion (Mark 15:39). The police who arrest Jesus are Jewish police (John 18:12).

Especially in John's Gospel, Jesus is distanced from "the Jews," as if he were not one of them by birth and by loyalty. Because of the opposition of the Pharisees to him, the author of the Gospel of John writes: "Jesus no longer walked about openly" (John 11:54), as if Jesus were not part of this group "Jews." In Matthew the Pharisees and scribes are consistently portrayed in a negative light. In all the Gospels, the Pharisees associate Jesus' miracle activity with demons (9:34, 12:24). The scribes think Jesus is blaspheming when he forgives sin (Matt 9:3). They have evil in their hearts. They test him (16:1). But a Gentile woman receives praise. A Canaanite woman who approaches him to heal her daughter is praised by Jesus when she challenges his initial refusal to help her on the grounds that his mission was only to Israel. "Then Jesus answered her, 'Woman, great is your faith! Let it be done for you as you wish'" (Matt 15:22–28).

Theologians of the first Christian centuries saw in the Gospels and in the letters of Paul one conclusion: the Jews killed Jesus. Given their belief in the identity of the risen Jesus with God, this became an accusation of deicide—killing God. This is the root of what is called Christian theological anti-Semitism.

The term *anti-Semitism* is a modern one. It denotes the racial hatred of Jews and has been most flagrantly practiced in their persecution and genocide by Adolf Hitler and Nazi Germany. It took historical form as the "final solution," in which Hitler set out to eliminate the Jewish population, murdering millions through a variety of violent means, including the gas chambers in concentration camps. The term is applied in retrospect to the negative attitudes of Christians about Jews. Theirs is primarily a religious or theological prejudice, not a racial one. Like any prejudice, it is an ideology of superiority, a mixture of the rational and irrational, and prone to violence. Christian anti-Semitism over two millennia set the stage for the Holocaust.

SUPERSESSIONISM

The messianic movement that had started out as Jewish in the early part of the first century was predominantly Gentile by the end of the century. Theologians in the early church struggled to formulate their relation to Jews and to the history of Israel. One answer that was influential by virtue of its simplicity and power in shaping the self-identity of Christians was this one: *we have replaced them.* The idea that Christianity had superseded Judaism and its covenant was enormously compelling to Christians.

One of the earliest ways of defining the beginning of Christianity, then, was in terms of the end of Judaism. Theologians drew contrasts that were subtle but effective ways of communicating the superiority of one and the inferiority of the other: Christianity over Judaism, Christ over Moses, gospel over law, church over synagogue.

Early church theologians villified and demonized the Jews. This language permeated the preaching and teaching of Christians. It is heard in liturgical prayers and read in theological treatises.[2] Statements like these became routine descriptions of Jewish and Christian identity:

- By rejecting Jesus, Jews forfeited their covenant with God.
- Christians have replaced Jews as God's elected ones.
- Christianity is the "new Israel."
- Judaism is a religion of "works righteousness."
- Jews thought they could merit salvation by doing works.
- Pharisees were legalistic, obsessed with the law.
- Jewish suffering is God's punishment for their refusal of Jesus.
- The Jews crucified God; they are guilty of deicide.

ELECTION

The caricature of Judaism as legalistic and as a religion of works righteousness militated against recognition of the authenticity of Jewish spirituality and the role of Torah observance in the life of covenant fidelity. Christians appropriated the language of election and covenant. They saw themselves as the new people of God. They replaced Israel's exclusivist religious self-understanding with their own. Now instead of observance of the law as a criterion of covenant fidelity, it is faith in Christ. Religious exclusivism, in either case, promotes the view that there is only one way of salvation. The Christian notion of salvation was exclusivist: there is one way—Christ. The exclusivism of ancient Israel could be expressed in the slogan, "Outside the law there is no salvation," meaning outside those who meet the condition

God has laid down for covenant fidelity—Torah observance.
No other religions can have salvific value if there is only one
right means of salvation offered by God. In the Christian
tradition, the mantra "Outside the Church there is no salvation" held firm until the twentieth century, when the
Second Vatican Council saw a ray of light in non-Christian
belief, including Judaism.

The primary problem with religious exclusivism—and
there are others—is that it heads straight for violence.
Those who do not agree with you must not be tolerated
but must be eliminated. We see a dramatic example of
this in the Hebrew Bible. The relation between Israel's
theology of election and violence is quite evident. The
biblical writers emphasize that Israel's election is due to
Yahweh's favor, not to Israel's merit (cf. Amos 3). Belief
must be exclusive and admit no other gods (Exod 20:1–2).
Whoever worships another god is to be destroyed (Exod
22:20; Deut 6:14–15). The cultural and religious other is
to be shown no mercy and annihilated; everything must be
destroyed in order that Israel's holiness not be contami-
nated (Deut 7:1–6). God is shown directing the violence
in all its tragic detail:

> Then the Lord said to [Moses], "See, I have begun to give
> [King] Sihon and his land over to you. Begin now to take
> possession of his land." So when Sihon came out against us,
> he and all his people, for battle at Jahaz, the LORD our God
> gave him over to us; and we struck him down, along with his
> offspring and all his people. At that time we captured all his
> towns, and in each town we utterly destroyed men, women,
> and children. We left not a single survivor. Only the livestock
> we kept as spoil for ourselves, as well as the plunder of the

towns that we had captured. . . . The LORD our God gave
everything to us. (Deut 2:31–36)

CHRISTIAN EXCLUSIVISM

The Jesus movement took over Israel's theology of election
and religious privilege.[3] For Jews, the criterion for righteousness was fidelity to the law God had given them. For
Christians, the criterion became belief in Jesus. An ethno-
centric theology of election became a Christocentric one:
"And there is salvation in no one else, for there is no other
name under heaven given among men by which we must
be saved" (Acts 4:12). Once the doctrine of original sin
had developed in the early centuries of the church, Christ's
forgiveness of the sin inherited from Adam and Eve was
considered necessary for salvation.[4] Because this forgiveness
is mediated sacramentally, by definition salvation requires
the mediation of the Church. This was summed up in
Cyprian's third-century exclusivist principle mentioned
above: "Outside the Church, there is no salvation."[5] The
Protestant version is Christocentric: "Outside Christ, there
is no salvation."[6]

The earliest stage of conflict over Jesus was the intra-
Jewish conflict between Jewish Jesus followers and Jews
who did not accept their messianic claims. The language is
polemical and bitter. The New Testament writers portray
the Pharisees as hypocritical and the scribes as corrupt. The
merely polemical character of the language was lost on later
Christians. It was understood simply as historical description: they were hypocritical, they were corrupt.

Paul's polemical language was uniformly misunderstood as well. Statements like these were interpreted as revelation of the inferiority and invalidity of Judaism:

- For all who rely on the works of the law are under a curse. (Gal 3:10)
- No one will be justified by the works of the law. (Gal 2:16)

Consistently misinterpreting Paul, the *adversus Judaeos* tradition put the Jews in the darkest of lights, as does John Chrysostom in the fourth century:

> Do not be surprised if I have called the Jews wretched and miserable for they have received many good things from God yet they have spurned them and violently cast them away. The sun of righteousness rose on them first, but they turned their back on its beams and sat in darkness. But we, who were nurtured in darkness, welcomed the light and we were freed from the yoke of error. The Jews were branches of the holy root, but they were lopped off. We were not part of the root, yet we have produced the fruits of piety. They read the prophets from ancient times, yet they crucified the one spoken of by the prophets. . . . They were called to sonship, but they degenerated to the level of dogs. . . . What sort of folly, what kind of madness, to participate in festivals of those who are dishonored, abandoned by God and provoked the Lord. . . . They killed the son of your Lord, and you dare to gather with them in the same place?[7]

Christian exclusivism could find no room for the integrity of other religions, especially Judaism. The sin of the

Jews lay in their failure to acknowledge Jesus as Messiah in the first century and refusing to convert to Christianity in the centuries that followed. Until it was removed from the liturgy by Pope John XXIII in 1959, this Good Friday prayer was heard by Catholics worldwide:

> Let us pray also for the unfaithful Jews, that our God and Lord may remove the veil from their hearts; that they also may acknowledge our Lord Jesus Christ. Almighty and everlasting God, Who drivest not even the faithless Jews away from Thy mercy, hear our prayers, which we offer for the blindness of that people, that, acknowledging the light of thy truth, which is Christ, they may be rescued from their darkness.[8]

Once Christianity became the religion of the empire after Constantine, Christian accusations of deicide and divine rejection against Jews justified denial of their social, political, economic, and religious rights, resulting in their marginalization and persecution.[9] The hostile language devaluing the Jews incited the violence of medieval pogroms. Martin Luther's advice to the German princes advocated a series of violent acts against the Jews. "What then shall we Christians do with this damned, rejected race of Jews?" he asked. His answer:

- Their synagogues should be set on fire.
- Their homes should be broken down and destroyed.
- They should be deprived of their prayer books and Talmuds.
- Their rabbis must be forbidden under threat of death to teach anymore.

- Passport and traveling privileges should be absolutely forbidden.
- They ought to be stopped from usury. . . . They have no other means of support.[10]

Like other books with such statements, today the volumes of Luther's work carry an apology to the Jews inside the front cover and an explanation in the introduction that Lutherans today do not share these views. Every Christian denomination has statements for which apologies have been necessary. With few exceptions, Christian denominations have issued public denunciations of supersessionist theology and statements such as Luther's that advocated violence or such as the Catholic prayer, which was oblivious to the reality and authenticity of Jewish spirituality.

The Christian proclamation of the Gospel has not been good news for the Jews. A religious ideology of superiority generated centuries of Christian hatred and violence against them, and social discrimination where possible. Rooted in the religious privilege assumed by the early Christians, the *adversus Judaeos* tradition ignored the redemptive insights of the Scriptures themselves—the prophetic call for justice and compassion for the vulnerable, Jesus' *basileia* vision of inclusion and his call for love of enemies, and the baptismal identification of religious privilege as sin. Even now the relation between Judaism and Christianity remains an unresolved theological problem.

Following the Second World War and the accusation that Christian theological anti-Semitism had prepared the way for the genocide undertaken by Adolf Hitler, Pauline scholars went back to Paul. What is called the "new perspective" is exactly that. Attention to the meaning of faith in Christ for Paul was at the center of the new perspective. Of the many scholarly insights over the past half century, these in particular have been important contributions:

- Paul joined a Jewish messianic movement, not a new religion.
- He did not know Christianity because it did not exist yet.
- Christianity and Judaism as distinct religions are a second-century phenomenon.
- Judaism was not a legalistic religion of works righteousness.
- "Doing works of the law" meant "living as a Jew."
- Paul did not believe Gentile inclusion in Israel's covenant required them to live as Jews.
- Paul did not reject Judaism or Torah observance for Jews.
- For Paul, faith and works were opposing conditions of membership in the Christ-confessing assembly, not ciphers for two religions.
- Faith in Christ is the means of salvation for both Jews and Gentiles.

These clarifications have been invaluable. But the theological worldview that results from changes in interpretation and meaning has been a difficult appropriation for some, especially where the dominance of Martin Luther's interpretation of the contrast between faith and works was shown to be quite distant from that of Paul himself. The challenge of removing the anti-Jewish bias from Christianity should not be underestimated. Johann-Baptist Metz captured the enormity of the task. After Auschwitz, he writes, "it is not a matter of a revision of Christian theology with regard to Judaism, but a matter of the revision of Christian theology itself."[11]

RECOVERING PAUL

The challenge of recovering the authentic Paul continues today. Questions change because we have new insights and the constellation of judgments creates a new context for interpretation. But the recovery of Paul requires, too, that we go beyond Paul to those who wrote in his name and the claims even of a whole tradition. Genuine recovery will restore Paul without the influence of Deutero-Pauline writers and the *adversus Judaeos* tradition.

This is harder than it sounds. Countless interpreters have presumed Paul to be what is found in Colossians, Ephesians, and 1 Timothy. They presumed he is the source of judgments of Judaism's invalidity and end and that God is his source. With these influences first in mind, subsequent interpretation can hardly be anything other than supersessionist.

We might be tempted to think that supersessionism is a problem just for ordinary people prone to bigotry, but it extends into every realm of Christian existence, including the realm of biblical scholarship. Those who pride themselves as the most objective in their understanding of Paul have often absorbed the polemical accusations of the *adversus Judaeos* tradition as God-given truths. For many shaped by this tradition, recovering Paul has first to do with eliminating what has been accepted as obvious and true.

We do not have to go far to find contributions to the *adversus Judaeos* tradition in the work of recent biblical scholars. What goes unnoticed in the technical work of exegesis—conducted under the watchwords of neutrality, objectivity, and verification—is the power that the confessional claims of their tradition have over scholars' interpretation of the data. For Lutherans, this has centered on the meaning and centrality that Martin Luther gave to Paul's concept of justification by faith.[12] I offer three examples.

Rudolph Bultmann

Bultmann may very well be the most famous of twentieth-century biblical scholars, known especially for his project of "demythologization" and insights into the existential meaning of the scriptures. As a starting point, however, he took the distinction deeply embedded in the tradition between faith in Christ and works of the law as signaling the superiority of Christianity over Judaism. He integrated all of the traditional criticisms into his thoroughly modern approach to the New Testament. For Bultmann, Magnus Zetterholm writes:

> Judaism was characterized by a far-reaching legalism, belief in a God that no longer acted in history, and a soteriological system based on merits, which leaves room for both religious hypocrisy and a feeling of uncertainty about one's relationship with God. According to Bultmann, this was exactly what Jesus reacted against, and is ultimately the religious system criticized in the Gospels.[13]

Ernst Käsemann

In his interpretation of Paul, Käsemann, another noted German biblical scholar, defended the traditional Lutheran teaching of justification by faith, arguing that Paul's concept of justification arose from conflict with Judaism and, further, that it was directed against Judaism. His presuppositions reflected classical Protestant theology, and his work repeated standard stereotypes: "Judaism represents legalism and the striving for self-justification, and Paul's theology is characterized by a radical criticism of the basis for Jewish piety—the Torah."[14]

Günther Bornkamm

Bornkamm, yet another German Lutheran biblical scholar, maintained Luther's opposition between the law and the Gospel, emphasizing that justification by faith was the center of Paul's theology. He argued that "Paul entirely rejects the ability of the law to lead anyone to salvation."[15] He rejected the religious life of the pious Jew, arguing that "the Jew is abandoned to God's wrath, beyond all salvation, while struggling to attain communication with him by means of the law."[16] For all three scholars, Paul had abandoned Judaism.

But, along with the routine acceptance of the *adversus Judaeos* tradition by some, challenges to the tradition were underway by others. We have already seen some of the results of this challenge. Krister Stendahl clarified that it was Martin Luther—not Paul—for whom justification by faith was central. It is important in Paul, but it is not the absolutely most central idea. Luther's cry that justification comes through faith alone, not through works, has more to do with his opposition to the abuses of the medieval Catholic Church and its control of sacramental access to God's grace. E. P. Sanders single-handedly cut through the caricatures of Judaism, the Pharisees, and Torah embedded in Christian teaching and preaching. He put to rest the accusation made of Judaism that it was guilty of works righteousness and legalism. James Dunn recovered the social meaning carried by the contrast between faith in Christ and works of the law and the way in which it functioned in the conflict in Galatia over membership. The contributions of others have been noted throughout this book.

NEW SCHOLARSHIP

Without the androcentrism of the Deutero-Pauline letters and the supersessionism of the interpreted Paul in the *adversus Judaeos* tradition, the data can be approached differently with new questions and different results. This is illustrated, for example, by Neil Elliott's work on Romans, a letter long thought to be the major source for Paul's critique and rejection of Judaism.[17] It was presumed that Paul's intention was twofold: to explain his gospel to Jewish Christians in Rome and to express his rejection of Judaism. Without the interference of supersessionist presuppositions, Elliott understood the data of the letter differently. He speculated that Paul was actually addressing the Gentile Christians, not the Jewish Christians. They were creating the problem with which Paul was concerned. Recall that the emperor Claudius exiled the Jews from

Rome in 49 C.E. because of disturbances and fighting in the synagogues and that Nero allowed them to return in 54 C.E. Paul is admonishing the Gentile members against "boasting" about their place in God's plan of salvation and against dismissing the Jewish members.

This kind of shift of perspective has taken place innumerable times in recent scholarship as dominant images controlling interpretation for centuries have been dropped. If, for example, there is no Christianity as a separate religion in Paul's time, then no matter what Paul is doing, he is doing it in the context of Judaism—or to be more precise, the Judaisms of the first century. Jewish scholar Alan Segal describes Paul this way: "Paul's letters record the thinking of a Pharisee who has converted to a new, apocalyptic, mystical, and—to many of his contemporaries—suspiciously heretical form of Judaism."[18]

QUESTIONS FOR
REFLECTION AND DISCUSSION

1. Just as Paul absorbed the Pharisaic worldview in his growing up as a Diaspora Jew, so, too, even in the modern era Christians have absorbed elements of the *adversus Judaeos* tradition. Is that true for your own experience? How? In what way?

2. What are two misunderstandings of early church theologians that led to a supersessionist tradition?

3. What is the difference between the way Paul understood the death of Jesus in relation to the Gentiles and the way early church theologians understood it?

4. James D. G. Dunn is noted for his recovery of the meaning of "works of the law" in first-century Judaism. How does this meaning change—for instance, in the use of "works righteousness"—in the Christian tradition?

8

Finding Paul

T he primary task we have undertaken in this work is to do what our title advocates: encounter Paul. Our access to Paul, as we have suggested in numerous ways, is not straightforward. Much of the influence attributed to Paul should be rightfully given to the Deutero-Pauline authors. But the good news is not that Paul is devalued as a consequence but that he is liberated from blame for what are, from our perspective today, morally objectionable views and scriptures.

It was the Deutero-Pauline writers, not Paul, who accepted slavery and maintained the lesser status of women. As their deliberate integration of the household codes suggests, these writers were engaged not in shaping emancipatory charismatic communities, as was Paul, but in the active reappropriation of patriarchal norms and structures for the *ekklēsia*. Theirs was not an accidental misunderstanding of Paul's notion of redemptive equality but a subversion of it. For Paul to proclaim, as did the writer of 1 Timothy, that women would be saved by childbearing would have necessitated a radical reversal of the way he thought of the justification of Gentile women.

The historical effects of the disputed letters have been tragic indeed. Brief passages legitimated ownership of slaves in the minds of Christians for nineteen centuries. Male theologians ignored the equality shown to women by Jesus and Paul to align Christian teaching with patriarchal views of women as property and as created for the purpose of reproduction. Christians engaged in harsh polemics against the Jews while defining Christianity by values such as love of neighbor and self-sacrificing love. The suffering of people under structures of domination has been undeniable and the scale of their suffering incalculable.

APPROPRIATING PAUL TODAY

In concluding, I return to a point made early on. After making these distinctions and the three Pauls that I have named, I do not end up somehow with a perfect historical Paul. Paul was a human being subject to the oversights, blind spots, and shortcomings that go with humanness. But for modern people whose world is evolutionary, perfection is not the ideal anyway. Becoming and self-realization are values. We are aware of how difficult authenticity is to achieve. Paul's letters show a man passionately dedicated to his message and mission and whose bumps and starts in the lifelong process of becoming who he was to become was right there for everyone to see. It is not only what we see in Paul that is of value but what we do not see as well. We do not find a dispassionate voice reducing human beings to property and dividing the redemptive community into privileged and nonprivileged spheres.

Encountering Paul requires turning to the past. A historically conscious reading seeks first to understand the social situation in which the text is located. But to encounter invites bringing Paul's letters into our context as well. They have significance for the present. We can be challenged by a man whose life was consumed by his immediate experience of the risen Christ. The problems with which Paul deals evoke questions for today. How are we shaping our institutions and lives by redemptive equality? What is being converted in us? What does the Spirit empower in our lives? How is holiness different than moral goodness?

Paul often asked the recipients of his letters to take him as a model for their lives. We can do so, too. He models bringing theological integrity and creativity to the problems, questions, and conflicts of our time. Like Paul, we have to think things out on the spot. We may find that the ethical overshadows the theological. No matter how we formulate the theological meaning of redemption, in the end redemption is performance. It is transformation through good of a world distorted by evil. The good is concrete, not abstract. We will discover it and see it on the move, so to speak. We have only this life, this day, and this moment to participate, as Bernard Lonergan puts it, in the realization of the universe. For God, this world is an ongoing judgment of value. We are cocreators in its realization. Encountering Paul inspires us to take on this task with renewed vigor and endless hope.

QUESTIONS FOR
REFLECTION AND DISCUSSION

1. Have the authors of the disputed letters helped or hurt Paul's reputation?

2. Looking over the whole book as a review, what are the distinctive features of the historical Paul that we find in his letters? Make a list of fifteen or so features.

3. Understanding Paul is different than just reading Paul. Has this book or this course and book been a source of encounter with Paul for you? What do you think of him? Could he be a model for you in your life? (Not in his polemical language, I hope!)

4. I ended this book by saying "redemption is performance. It is transformation with good of a world distorted by evil." Have you been part of the performance? How?

Notes

PREFACE

1. Unless otherwise noted, biblical texts are from the New Revised Standard Version, in Michael D. Coogan, ed., *The New Oxford Annotated Bible*, 3rd ed. (Oxford: Oxford University Press, 2001).

2. These are topics and claims I will substantiate in the following chapters.

3. Peter Garnsey, *Ideas of Slavery from Aristotle to Augustine* (Cambridge: Cambridge University Press, 1996).

4. Quoted in Eusebius, *History of the Church*, trans. Paul Maier (Grand Rapids, Mich.: Kregel, 1999), 6.25, 3–14.

5. Johann-Baptist Metz, "Facing the Jews: Christian Theology after Auschwitz," in Elisabeth Schüssler Fiorenza and David Tracy, eds., *The Holocaust as Interruption*, Concilium 175:5 (Edinburgh: T & T Clark, 1984), 26–33; 27.

CHAPTER 1

1. John Painter, *Just James: The Brother of Jesus in History and Tradition* (Minneapolis: Fortress Press, 1999), 48; 56.

2. We draw from a number of respected sources throughout the book. Among them, especially important for this chapter, is Larry W. Hurtado, *Lord Jesus Christ: Devotion to Jesus in Earliest Christianity* (Grand Rapids, Mich.: Eerdmans, 2003); and Ekkehard W. Stegemann and Wolfgang Stegemann, *The Jesus Movement: A Social History of Its First Century* (Minneapolis: Fortress Press, 1999). At the center of influential books that changed the way Jesus and Paul are understood in relation to their Jewish context, not to say the context itself, is E. P. Sanders's *Paul and Palestinian Judaism* (Philadelphia: Fortress Press, 1977); and idem, *Jesus and Judaism* (Philadelphia: Fortress Press, 1976). See also idem, *Paul: A Very Short Introduction* (Oxford: Oxford University Press, 2001), a useful work for our purposes here. Another important source is James D. G. Dunn, *The Cambridge Companion to Paul* (Cambridge: Cambridge University Press, 2003); and James D. G. Dunn, *The Theology of Paul the Apostle* (Edinburgh: T & T Clark, 1998). The leading feminist biblical scholar who has shed much light on Jesus, Christian origins, and Paul, is Elisabeth Schüssler Fiorenza. See *The Power of the Word: Scripture and the Rhetoric of Empire* (Minneapolis: Fortress Press, 2007). Her now-classic work on women and the Pauline assembly as a "discipleship community of equals" is found in *In Memory of Her: A Feminist Theological Reconstruction of Christian Origins* (New York: Crossroad, 1987), 107.

3. See Sarah J. Tanzer, "Judaisms of the First Century C.E.," in *The Oxford Companion to the Bible*, Bruce M. Metzger and Michael D. Coogan, eds. (Oxford: Oxford University Press, 1993). Accessed online June 2, 2009: http://www.oxfordreference.com/views/ENTRY.html?subview=Main&entry=t120.e0394.

4. On the Hebrew Bible, see the articles in Metzger and Coogan, eds., *The Oxford Companion to the Bible*, by Gary N. Knoppers ("Israel"), R. N. Whybray ("Tribes of Israel"), and J. Maxwell Miller ("Judah, The Kingdom of" and "Israel, History of"). Accessed online June 1, 2009: http://www.oxfordreference.com/views/ENTRY.html?subview=Main&entry=t120.e0355.

5. Walter Wink, *Engaging the Powers: Discernment and Resistance in a World of Domination* (Minneapolis: Fortress Press, 1992), esp. 51–107.

6. K. C. Hanson and Douglas Oakman, *Palestine in the Time of Jesus: Social Structures and Social Conflicts* (Minneapolis: Fortress Press, 1998), 87.

7. Howard Clark Kee et al., eds., *The Cambridge Companion to the Bible* (Cambridge: Cambridge University Press, 2008), 359–62.

8. On Paul and empire, see Wolfgang Stegemann, Bruce J. Malina, and Gerd Theissen, eds., *The Social Setting of Jesus and the Gospels* (Minneapolis: Fortress Press, 2002). An important contributor to understanding Paul in relation to the Roman Empire is Neil Elliott, *Liberating Paul: The Justice of God and the Politics of the Apostle* (Minneapolis: Fortress Press, 2006 [1994]); and Neil Elliott, *The Arrogance of Nations: Reading Romans in the Shadow of Empire* (Minneapolis: Fortress Press, 2008).

9. On crucifixion, see Hanson and Oakman, *Palestine,* 90–95. This book is also a resource for the topic of religion and empire addressed below.

10. Placing Paul in the context of the Roman Empire is a recent emphasis in Pauline scholarship. In addition to the works cited above, see John Dominic Crossan and Jonathan Reed, *In Search of Paul: How Jesus' Apostle Opposed Rome's Empire with God's Kingdom* (San Francisco: HarperSanFrancisco, 2004).

11. The term *social death* is Orlando Patterson's. See his *Slavery and Social Death: A Comparative Study* (Cambridge, Mass.: Harvard University Press, 1982).

12. Hurtado, *Lord Jesus Christ,* 138; see p. 117 on Jesus' status.

CHAPTER 2

1. Valuable resources for this chapter include: Gerd Theissen and Annette Merz, *The Historical Jesus: A Comprehensive Guide* (Minneapolis: Fortress Press, 1998); Alan F. Segal, *Paul the Convert: The Apostolate and Apostasy of Saul the Pharisee* (New Haven, Conn.: Yale University Press, 1992); Alan F. Segal, *Rebecca's Children: Judaism and Christianity in the Roman World* (Cambridge, Mass.: Harvard University

Press, 1986), 112–13; E. P. Sanders, *Jesus and Judaism* (Philadelphia: Fortress Press, 1976); Sidnie White Crawford, "Apocalyptic," and James R. Mueller, "Pseudepigrapha," in David Noel Freedman et al., eds., *Eerdmans Dictionary of the Bible* (Grand Rapids, Mich.: Eerdmans, 2000), 72–73 and 1096–97, respectively.

2. Theissen and Merz, *The Historical Jesus*, 240–80; esp. 275–76.

3. See Crawford, "Apocalyptic," 72–73; and Mueller, "Pseudepigrapha," 1096–97.

4. On Jesus' preaching, see Tatha Wiley, "Creation Restored: God's *Basileia*, the Social Economy, and the Human Good," in Carol Dempsey and Mary Margaret Pazden, eds., *Earth, Wind, and Fire: Biblical and Theological Perspectives on Creation* (Collegeville, Minn.: Liturgical Press, 2004), 77–102. Stephen Patterson emphasizes the translation of *basileia* as *empire* in *The God of Jesus: The Historical Jesus and the Search for Meaning* (New York: Continuum International, 1998), 60–61.

5. Walter Wink, *Engaging the Powers: Discernment and Resistance in a World of Domination* (Minneapolis: Fortress Press, 1992), 51.

6. Wink, *Engaging the Powers*, 107.

7. David Brondos, *Paul on the Cross: Reconstructing the Apostle's Story of Redemption* (Minneapolis: Fortress Press, 2006).

8. Brondos, *Paul on the Cross*, 175.

9. Richard A. Horsley and Neil Asher Silberman, *The Message and the Kingdom: How Jesus and Paul Ignited a Revolution and Transformed the Ancient World* (Minneapolis: Fortress Press, 2002 [1997]), 32. John the Baptist is discussed on pp. 32–34.

10. Segal, *Rebecca's Children*, 108.

11. E. P. Sanders, *Paul, the Law, and the Jewish People* (Minneapolis: Fortress Press, 1983), 207.

12. See Segal, *Rebecca's Children*, 113, for the difficulties with Paul's conception of Gentile conversion. Paul's was the minority position in the Jesus movement. On James, see John Painter, *Just James: The Brother of Jesus in History and Tradition* (Minneapolis: Fortress Press, 1999), 49.

13. On Galatians 3:28 as a pre-Pauline baptismal fragment, see Hans Dieter Betz, *Galatians*, Hermeneia (Philadelphia: Fortress Press, 1979), 181–201.

14. Elisabeth Schüssler Fiorenza, "Women in the Early Christian Movement," in Carol P. Christ and Judith Plaskow, eds., *Womanspirit Rising: A Feminist Reader in Religion* (San Francisco: HarperSanFrancisco, 1992), 84–92; 88.

15. Larry W. Hurtado, *Lord Jesus Christ: Devotion to Jesus in Earliest Christianity* (Grand Rapids, Mich.: Eerdmans, 2003), 106, n. 67.

16. James D. G. Dunn, *Unity and Diversity in the New Testament: An Inquiry into the Character of Earliest Christianity* (London: SCM Press, 2006), 111. See also pp. 190–91.

CHAPTER 3

1. For an overview of Paul's thought with discussion of scholarly differences, see, all by David G. Horrell, "The Heart of Paul's Theology: Central Themes," in John Barton, ed., *The Biblical World* (New York: Routledge, 2000), available at Routledge Reference Resources online: http://www.reference.routledge.com/subscriber/entry?entry=w001_w001b42.5; "Paul's Call to Apostleship and Missionary Activity," http://www.reference.routledge.com/subscriber/entry?entry=w001_w001b42.4; "Paul's Legacy," http://www.reference.routledge.com/subscriber/entry?entry=w001_w001b42.6. Accessed January 5, 2009.

2. In addition to works by Betz, Dunn, Hurtado, Kee, Painter, Sanders, Stegemann and Stegemann, Schüssler Fiorenza, and Segal, cited in earlier chapters, resources for this chapter include Shaye J. D. Cohen, "Conversion to Judaism in Historical Perspective: From Biblical Israel to Postbiblical Judaism," *Conservative Judaism* 36 (1983): 31–45.

3. Larry W. Hurtado, *Lord Jesus Christ: Devotion to Jesus in Earliest Christianity* (Grand Rapids, Mich.: Eerdmans, 2003), 161.

4. John Painter, *Just James: The Brother of Jesus in History and Tradition* (Minneapolis: Fortress Press, 1999), 56.

5. E. P. Sanders, *Paul and Palestinian Judaism: A Comparison of Patterns of Religion* (Philadelphia: Fortress Press, 1977), 441.

6. See Alan F. Segal, *Paul the Convert: The Apostolate and Apostasy of Saul the Pharisee* (New Haven: Yale University Press, 1992), 117; Calvin J. Roetzel, *Paul: The Man and the Myth* (Minneapolis: Fortress Press, 1999), 46–47.

7. See Elisabeth Schüssler Fiorenza, *The Power of the Word: Scripture and the Rhetoric of Empire* (Minneapolis: Fortress Press, 2007), 71–72.

8. Elisabeth Schüssler Fiorenza, "Women in the Early Christian Movement," in Carol P. Christ and Judith Plaskow, eds., *Womanspirit Rising: A Feminist Reader in Religion* (San Francisco: HarperSan Francisco, 1992), 88.

9. James D. G. Dunn, "Prolegomena to a Theology of Paul," *New Testament Studies* 40 (1994): 407–32.

10. James D. G. Dunn, *Jesus, Paul and the Law: Studies in Mark and Galatians* (Louisville: Westminster John Knox Press, 1990), 193.

11. Pheme Perkins, *Gnosticism and the New Testament* (Minneapolis: Fortress Press, 1993), 166.

CHAPTER 4

1. Calvin J. Roetzel, *Paul: The Man and the Myth* (Minneapolis: Fortress Press, 1999), 2.

2. Biblical references in this chapter are to the Letter to the Galatians unless otherwise noted.

3. Roetzel, *Paul*, 11.

4. E. P. Sanders, *Paul, the Law, and the Jewish People* (Minneapolis: Fortress Press, 1983), 19.

5. Cf. the texts quoted below: Deut. 11:12–16, 26–28; and 26:16–19.

6. On the uncertainty of the location of the Galatian churches, see Wayne Meeks, *The First Urban Christians: The Social World of Apostle Paul*, 2nd ed. (New Haven, Conn.: Yale University Press, 2003), 42–43.

7. Fear of circumcision, at least among men, was not the only factor keeping Gentiles at the stage of sympathizers or God fearers, rather than fully converted proselytes. There was also the political obligation to worship local deities as well as the imperial cult, an obligation from which those born Jews were exempt but converts to Judaism were not. They could be charged with "atheism" if they failed to worship as obliged to

do. Louis H. Feldman, "Jewish Proselytism," in Harold W. Attridge and Gohei Hata, eds., *Eusebius, Christianity, and Judaism* (Detroit: Wayne State University Press, 1992), 372–408. On Gentile God fearers and proselytes as early converts to messianic Judaism, see James D. G. Dunn, *The Parting of the Ways: Between Christianity and Judaism and Their Significance for the Character of Christianity* (Philadelphia: Trinity Press International, 1991), 125–33; and Alan Segal, *Rebecca's Children: Judaism and Christianity in the Roman World* (Cambridge, Mass.: Harvard University Press, 1986), 96–98. On women converts to Judaism, see Ross Shepard Kraemer, *Her Share of the Blessings: Women's Religions among Pagans, Jews, and Christians in the Greco-Roman World* (New York: Oxford University Press, 1992).

8. Feldman, "Jewish Proselytism," 387.

9. Larry Hurtado, *Lord Jesus Christ: Devotion to Jesus in Earliest Christianity* (Grand Rapids, Mich.: Eerdmans, 2003), 161.

10. E. P. Sanders, *Paul and Palestinian Judaism: A Comparison of Patterns of Religion* (Philadelphia: Fortress Press, 1977), 206.

11. E. P. Sanders, *Jesus and Judaism* (Philadelphia: Fortress Press, 1976), 56–57 (italics in text).

12. Elisabeth Schüssler Fiorenza, *Discipleship of Equals: A Feminist Ekklesialogy of Liberation* (New York: Crossroad, 1993). See also Meeks, *First Urban Christians*, 30.

13. See, e.g., Alister E. McGrath, *Christianity: An Introduction* (New York: Wiley-Blackwell, 2006), 347–48.

14. Elisabeth Schüssler Fiorenza, *In Memory of Her: A Feminist Theological Reconstruction of Christian Origins* (New York: Crossroad, 1984).

15. Karen Jo Torjesen, "Reconstruction of Women's Early Christian History," in Elisabeth Schüssler Fiorenza et al., eds., *Searching the Scriptures*, vol. 1 (New York: Crossroad, 1993), 290–331; 294–95.

16. Bernadette J. Brooten, *Women Leaders in the Ancient Synagogue* (Chico, Calif.: Scholars Press, 1982), 150.

17. Shaye Cohen, "Women in the Synagogues of Antiquity," *Conservative Judaism* 34 (1980): 23–29; 24.

18. Kraemer, *Her Share of the Blessings*, 93.

19. John Painter, *Just James: The Brother of Jesus in History and Tradition* (Minneapolis: Fortress Press, 1999), 49.

20. On the meaning of *works of the law*, see James D. G. Dunn, "Prolegomena to a Theology of Paul," *New Testament Studies* 40 (1994): 407–32.

21. Women are not obliged to perform commandments that must be performed at a specific time, presumably because they would interfere with household duties. The three positive commandments specifically assigned to women are separating a piece of dough from the kneading bowl to give to the priests at Hallah, lighting the Sabbath candles, and upholding the laws of family purity. "Women," in Geoffrey Wigoder, ed., *The Encyclopedia of Judaism* (New York: Macmillan, 1989), 732–34.

22. See James D. G. Dunn, "Yet Once More—'The Works of the Law': A Response," *Journal for the Study of the New Testament* 46 (1992): 99–117.

23. Sanders, *Paul and Palestinian Judaism*, 83–84, 206–12. Salvation is promised to those in the covenant. Thus the concern, as we will see, with the issue of membership, i.e., getting in and staying in (212).

24. James D. G. Dunn, *The Epistle to the Galatians*, Black's New Testament Commentary (Peabody, Mass.: Hendrickson, 1993), 127.

25. See Tatha Wiley, *Paul and the Gentile Women: Reframing Galatians* (New York: Continuum, 2005).

26. Schüssler Fiorenza, *In Memory of Her*, 210.

27. Kraemer, *Her Share of the Blessings*, 96.

28. Kraemer, *Her Share of the Blessings*, 105.

29. Judith Romney Wegner, *Chattel or Person? The Status of Women in the Mishnah* (New York: Oxford University Press, 1988), 150.

30. Wegner, *Chattel or Person?*, 14–50.

31. Kraemer, *Her Share of the Blessings*, 100.

CHAPTER 5

1. Calvin J. Roetzel, *Paul: The Man and the Myth* (Minneapolis: Fortress Press, 1999), 44–47.

2. Roetzel, *Paul*, 6.

3. Anthony J. Saldarini, "Pharisees," in David N. Freedman, ed., *Anchor Bible Dictionary*, vol. 5 (New York: Doubleday), 289–303.

4. E. P. Sanders, *Paul and Palestinian Judaism: A Comparison of Patterns of Religion* (Philadelphia: Fortress Press, 1977), 233.

5. James D. G. Dunn, "The Theology of Galatians: The Issue of Covenantal Nomism," in Jouette M. Bassler, ed., *Pauline Theology: Vol. 1. Thessalonians, Philippians, Galatians, Philemon* (Minneapolis: Fortress Press, 1991), 125–46; 128. See also James D. G. Dunn, "Yet Once More—'The Works of the Law': A Response," *Journal for the Study of the New Testament* 46 (1992): 99–117.

6. Dunn, "Yet Once More," 100.

7. James D. G. Dunn, *The Epistle to the Galatians*, Black's New Testament Commentary (Peabody, Mass.: Hendrickson, 1993), 266–71.

8. Elisabeth Schüssler Fiorenza, "Women in the Pre-Pauline and Pauline Churches," *Union Seminary Quarterly Review* 33 (1978): 153–66; 155.

9. Helpful resources for the letters are Calvin J. Roetzel, *The Letters of Paul: Conversations in Context*, 4th ed. (Louisville: Westminster John Knox Press, 1998); and Leander Keck, *Paul and His Letters*, 2nd ed. (Philadelphia: Fortress Press, 1988).

10. See, for example, Richard A. Horsley and Neil Asher Silberman, *The Message and the Kingdom: How Jesus and Paul Ignited a Revolution and Transformed the Ancient World* (Minneapolis: Fortress Press, 2002 [1997]).

11. Keck, *Paul and His Letters*, 76, 78.

12. E. P. Sanders emphasized Paul's notion of participation and identification with Christ. See *Paul and Palestinian Judaism: A Comparison of Patterns of Religion* (Philadelphia: Fortress Press, 1977), 467–68.

13. A summary is given by Frank J. Matera in "Galatians in Perspective," *Interpretation* 54, no. 3 (2000): 233–45. The term is James Dunn's. See James D. G. Dunn, "The New Perspective on Paul," *Bulletin of the John Rylands Library* 65 (1983): 95–122.

14. See Tatha Wiley, *Paul and the Gentile Women: Reframing Galatians* (New York: Continuum, 2005).

15. James D. G. Dunn, *The Theology of Paul's Letter to the Galatians* (Cambridge: Cambridge University Press, 1993), 50.

16. Romans 16 has been questioned as part of the original manuscript. It is missing in some of the oldest versions. But in the judgment of Elizabeth A. Castelli, Romans 16 is genuine Pauline material and belongs to the letter. See her "Romans," in Elisabeth Schüssler Fiorenza, ed., *Searching the Scriptures: A Feminist Commentary*, vol. 2 (New York: Crossroad, 1994), 276–80.

17. A helpful online resource for Paul is "Chapter Forty-One: Paul," in John Barton, ed., *The Biblical World* (New York: Routledge, 2002), available in Routledge Reference Resources online, Taylor & Francis Publishing Group, accessed March 15, 2009: http://www.reference.routledge.com/subscriber/entry?entry=w001_w001b42.

18. Roetzel, *Paul.*

19. Peter Lampe, *From Paul to Valentinus: Christians at Rome in the First Two Centuries,* trans. Michael Steinhauser, ed. Marshall D. Johnson (Minneapolis: Fortress Press, 2003), 11.

20. In a dense urban area such as Rome, Jesus followers met in apartment—tenement—buildings as well as houses. Lampe, *From Paul to Valentinus,* 46, 56, 63–66.

CHAPTER 6

1. The form-critical judgment is that Gal 3:28 is a pre-Pauline baptismal fragment. See Hans Dieter Betz, *Galatians*, Hermeneia (Philadelphia: Fortress Press, 1979), 181–85.

2. For an analysis of this household code, see Sarah J. Tanzer, "Ephesians," in Elisabeth Schüssler Fiorenza, ed., *Searching the Scriptures: A Feminist Commentary*, vol. 2 (New York: Crossroad, 1994), 325–48.

3. Cynthia Briggs Kittredge, "Pauline Texts," in Letty M. Russell and J. Shannon Clarkson, *Dictionary of Feminist Theologies* (Louisville: Westminster John Knox Press, 1996), 207–209; 207. In this same resource, see also Bonnie Thurston, "Pastoral Letters," 203–204, and Rosemary Radford Ruether, "Patriarchy," 205–206.

4. Kittredge, "Pauline Texts," 208.

5. Ross S. Kraemer, *Her Share of the Blessings: Women's Religions among Pagans, Jews, and Christians in the Greco-Roman World* (New York: Oxford University Press, 1992), 100. Kraemer writes that the right to observe the law and its denial create "separate and unequal spheres for women and men" (105). The Deutero-Pauline authors are engaged in something similar, not by way of the law but through appeal to the household codes from the culture. I am indebted to Kraemer for this term.

6. Karen Jo Torjesen, "Reconstruction of Women's Early Christian History," in Elisabeth Schüssler Fiorenza, *Searching the Scriptures: A Feminist Introduction* (New York: Crossroad, 1993), vol. 1, 290–310; 291–92.

7. Thurston, "Pastoral Letters," 203–204; 204.

8. Thurston, "Pastoral Letters," 203–204.

9. Thurston, "Pastoral Letters," 203–204.

10. Ronald D. Witherup, S.S., *101 Questions and Answers on Paul* (New York: Paulist Press, 2003), 13.

11. As the footnote in the Oxford NRSV Bible indicates, the prohibition of women's leadership in worship in 1 Cor 14:33–36 is likely an interpolation, a passage added by a later editor. Scholars raise the question whether 11:2–16, discussed below, is an interpolation, too.

12. Bernard Lonergan, *Method in Theology* (New York: Herder & Herder, 1972), 242–43.

13. Patterson is responsible for a significant change in how historians understand slave states and systems, especially the violence involved in maintaining slavery. See Orlando Patterson, *Slavery and Social Death: A Comparative Study* (Cambridge, Mass.: Harvard University Press, 1982).

14. Richard Horsley, "The Slave Systems of Classical Antiquity," in Allen Dwight Callahan et al., eds., *Semeia 83–84: Slavery in Text and Interpretation* (Atlanta: Scholars Press, 2001), esp. 38–45.

15. Jennifer A. Glancy, *Slavery in Early Christianity* (Minneapolis: Fortress Press, 2006). See especially chapter 2, "Body Work and the Pauline Churches," 39–70.

16. The Roman imperial elite were well aware of the economics of slavery. See Horsley, "The Slave Systems of Classical Antiquity," esp. 31–36.

17. Aristotle, *Politics* I.3–7; cf. Aristotle, *Nicomachean Ethics* VII.

18. E. Brooks Holifield, review of Jeffrey Robert Young, *Domesticating Slavery: The Master Class in Georgia and South Carolina* (Chapel Hill: University of North Carolina Press, 1999), in *Church History* 70 (2001): 810–11.

19. See David M. Potter, "The Work of Ulrich B. Phillips: A Comment," *Agricultural History* 41 (1967), 359–64.

20. See the discussion of royal consciousness in Walter Brueggemann, *The Prophetic Imagination*, 2nd ed. (Minneapolis: Fortress Press, 2001), esp. 21–37. A particularly harsh book blaming Christianity for slavery is Forrest G. Wood, *The Arrogance of Faith: Christianity and Race in America from the Colonial Era to the Twentieth Century* (New York: Alfred A. Knopf, 1990).

21. Augustine, *City of God*, 19:1.

22. See Aristotle, *Politics*, Book I, 3–5 [1253b–1255a], in Richard McKeon, ed., *The Basic Works of Aristotle* (New York: Random House, 1941), 1130–33.

23. See Thomas Aquinas, *Summa theologiae*, II/II, Q. 57, a. 3, "On Justice."

24. James Newton Poling, *Deliver Us from Evil: Resisting Racial and Gender Oppression* (Minneapolis: Fortress Press, 1996), 54; 12.

25. Poling, *Deliver Us from Evil*, 42.

26. Jack White, *Time*, March 7, 1995, 29.

CHAPTER 7

1. On the "truth of the gospel," see the excursus on Galatians in Calvin J. Roetzel, *Paul: The Man and the Myth* (Minneapolis: Fortress Press, 1999), 113.

2. This quote and others below from the tradition are from Mary C. Boys, *Has God Only One Blessing? Judaism as a Source of Christian Self-Understanding* (New York: Paulist Press, 2000). See, for example, pp. 8 and 76–79. Boys suggests ways of replacing supersessionism on p. 268. We must learn to hear the supersessionism embedded in Christian preaching and teaching. Boys gives the example of hearing this hymn: "O come, O come Emmanuel and ransom *captive Israel, that mourns*

in lonely exile here until the Son of God appears." The italicized lyrics, as Boys points out, imply that Judaism is obsolete; it lies in darkness (267).

3. For the development of Christian religious exclusivism and the *adversus Judaeos* tradition, I draw from John T. Pawlikowski, O.S.M., "The Christ Event and the Jewish People," in Tatha Wiley, ed., *Thinking of Christ: Proclamation, Explanation, Meaning* (New York: Continuum, 2003), 103–21; John T. Pawlikowski, "Christian Redemption between Colonialism and Pluralism," in Rebecca S. Chopp and Mark Lewis Taylor, eds., *Reconstructing Christian Theology* (Minneapolis: Fortress Press, 1994), 269–302.

4. See Tatha Wiley, *Original Sin: Origins, Developments, Contemporary Meanings* (New York: Paulist Press, 2002). The proclamation of Christ's redemption preceded and generated the doctrine of original sin. The doctrine answers the question why the need for Christ's forgiveness is universal.

5. Cyprian, *De cathol. eccl., unit.* 6.

6. The Christian exclusivism of Karl Barth, the influential twentieth-century theologian, was transparent: God's true revelation is given to Christianity. There is one Savior, Jesus; one true religion, Christianity; one means of salvation, the church. Karl Barth's stance is discussed in James C. Livingston et al., *Modern Christian Thought: The Twentieth Century,* 2nd ed. (Minneapolis: Fortress Press, 2002), 471–72.

7. John Chrysostom (d. 407 C.E.), "Homily One against the Jews." Cited on p. 56 in Boys, *Has God Only One Blessing?*

8. Cited on pp. 19 and 203 in Boys, *Has God Only One Blessing?*

9. Social and political control came to the church after the conversion of Constantine in 313 C.E. and the integration of Christianity into the imperial order. On official discrimination against the Jews, see pp. 58–59 in Boys, *Has God Only One Blessing?*

10. Martin Luther, *The Jews and Their Lies* (1542). Cited in Dan Cohn-Sherbok, *The Crucified Jew: Twenty Centuries of Christian Anti-Semitism* (London: HarperCollins Religious, 1992), 73.

11. Johann-Baptist Metz, "Facing the Jews: Christian Theology after Auschwitz," in Elisabeth Schüssler Fiorenza and David Tracy, eds., *The Holocaust as Interruption,* Concilium 175 (Edinburgh: T & T Clark, 1984), 26–33; 27.

12. On recent scholarship, I draw from Magnus Zetterholm, *Approaches to Paul: A Student's Guide to Recent Scholarship* (Minneapolis: Fortress Press, 2009), esp. 69–93.

13. Zetterholm, *Approaches to Paul*, 74.

14. Zetterholm, *Approaches to Paul*, 80.

15. Zetterholm, *Approaches to Paul*, 82.

16. Zetterholm, *Approaches to Paul*, 3.

17. Neil Elliott, *The Rhetoric of Romans: Argumentative Constraint and Strategy, and Paul's Dialogue with Judaism* (Minneapolis: Fortress Press, 2009 [1990]), 5. The following points are made on pp. 43, 59, and 67.

18. Alan Segal, *Paul the Pharisee: The Apostolate and Apostasy of Saul the Pharisee* (New Haven, Conn.: Yale University Press, 1992), xiii.

Index